"A painfully gorgeous journey i̇nto shamanism. 'Shedding the Layers warrior spirit in overcoming impossible odds, not just to reclaim one's health, but the miracle of living."

Jonathan Talat Phillips,
author of "The Electric Jesus: The Healing Journey of a Contemporary Gnostic", co-founder of Evolver.net & Reality Sandwich

"Mark's healing journey is worth reading, and his spiritual realizations are worth knowing—for all of us. 'Shedding the Layers' makes a valuable contribution to the literature on shamanic healing."

Chris Kilham,
The Medicine Hunter

"Flaherty reminds us that living from the heart is not just the only path worth taking, it's the only real medicine."

Adam Elenbaas,
author of "Fishers of Men: The Gospel of an Ayahuasca Vision Quest," and contributing editor at RealitySandwich.com

"This is a story of ultimate soul triumph: the twists and turns of the hero's journey."

Mags MacKean,
author of "Meetings On The Edge"

Shedding the Layers

How Ayahuasca Saved More Than My Skin

BY MARK FLAHERTY

Copyright © Mark Flaherty, 2012

All rights reserved. No part of this book may be reproduced, scanned, or distributed in any printed or electronic form without written permission from the copyright holder.

Cover artwork: *Uña de Gato* by Mimi Buttacavoli:
www.mimibuttacavoli.com
The head medicine spirit of Uña de Gato is a black jaguar, which extracts unwanted energies from the body.

Icaro lyrics © Chris Odle, 2012

ISBN 978-1470017330

Printed in the United States of America

The ideas, procedures and suggestions contained in this book are not intended as a substitute for consulting with a doctor. All matters regarding your health require medical supervision. Neither the author nor the publisher shall not be liable or responsible for any loss or damage arising from any information or suggestion in this book.

This is a true story. Some names have been changed to protect privacy.

ACKNOWLEDGMENTS

Firstly, I would like to thank Hamilton Souther for his tireless help, patience, generosity and extraordinary shamanic abilities. Thank you also to Don Alberto Torres Dávila, an exceptional master shaman with total dedication to his medicine practice. Without both of you, I would not be alive today. The gratitude and love I have for you and the work you do is boundless.

In addition, thank you to all the other shamanic workers who helped me through the long, arduous process of healing and transformation: Chris Odle, Mimi Buttacavoli, Mal Rossiter and Kellee Morris.

To my wonderful mom and dad, thank you for supporting me when I was too sick to look after myself and for putting up with my foul moods for so long.

Many people helped bring this book into existence. A heartfelt thank you goes to my fantastic editor, Libby Mulitz, for her dedication and countless hours of hard work in shaping my words into something publishable. Thanks also to my friends who were kind enough to take the time to read the drafts and provide invaluable feedback: Nicolai Ordahl, Rachel Sambrooks, Mags Mackean, Heather Delabre and Mark Conn.

I would also like to thank the staff, past and present, at Blue Morpho who work tirelessly and with much joy in helping provide life-changing experiences to so many.

Finally, thank you to the hundreds of wonderful Blue Morpho guests whom I've met over the last seven years. Many of you only know me from when I was miserably unsociable—it was nothing personal. While there are too many of you to name individually, I trust that you know who you are, and I thank you for your kindness, generosity and the amazing experiences we shared. I honour your commitment to growth and personal transformation.

CONTENTS

INTRODUCTION	(Walsall)	1
CHAPTER 1	The Search Begins (Cusco)	2
CHAPTER 2	Into the Other World (Iquitos)	13
CHAPTER 3	LSD and Witchcraft (Zambia)	34
CHAPTER 4	A Year in Bed (Walsall)	43
CHAPTER 5	The First Thirty Years	61
CHAPTER 6	Ayahuasca—Ultimate Hope (Iquitos)	72
CHAPTER 7	Into the Abyss (Iquitos)	85
CHAPTER 8	A Well-Earned Holiday (Walsall)	103
CHAPTER 9	Dark Night of the Soul (Walsall)	110
CHAPTER 10	Following the Call of the Medicine (Iquitos)	121
CHAPTER 11	Struggling with Growth (Iquitos)	131
CHAPTER 12	A Different Approach to Life (Walsall)	144
CHAPTER 13	Epiphany (Iquitos)	160
CHAPTER 14	The Search Ends with a New Journey (Walsall)	179

"To love at all is to be vulnerable. Love anything, and your heart will certainly be wrung and possibly broken. If you want to make sure of keeping it intact, you must give your heart to no one, not even to an animal. Wrap it carefully round with hobbies and little luxuries; avoid all entanglements; lock it up safe in the casket or coffin of your selfishness. But in that casket—safe, dark, motionless, airless—it will change. It will not be broken; it will become unbreakable, impenetrable, irredeemable."

C.S. Lewis

INTRODUCTION

May 2005

The face looking back at me in the mirror is a snarl of bloody, cracked skin, oozing a foul-smelling yellow liquid that trickles unchecked down its cheeks. The eyes are lifeless and defeated after months of agony. All features are frozen in place by the knowledge that the slightest twitch of the mouth or arch of an eyebrow is enough to split the skin open once more.

I consider the daunting tasks ahead of me: putting on clothes, walking downstairs, eating breakfast and returning to my room for another session of mindless daytime TV. I sigh and look down at the floor, littered with layers of dead skin. No matter how much I vacuum it's impossible to keep it clean.

As I do every morning, I inspect my body, hoping to find any evidence that this torture will end. My neck and chest are as diseased as my face. My arms and hands, also throbbing and bruised-purple like my face, are getting worse. They're etched with deep, infected cuts and inflamed scratch marks, casualties of the interminable itching.

This is my life—a moment-by-moment struggle to survive with severe eczema.

I take a deep breath and reach for the nearest shirt.

CHAPTER 1
The Search Begins

Eight months earlier

Just off the sixteen-hour bus ride from Nazca, I stagger into the Cusco station, barely able to keep my eyes open, my clothes a wrinkled mess. The twisting mountain roads jolted me awake every few minutes, my head lolling across the centre aisle or dangling precariously close to the ample lap of the Peruvian *campesina* lady next to me. Now I know why the local women always wear those long skirts. Seeing that the bus had no toilet, all passengers would periodically line up along the side to relieve themselves.

Like the vast majority of travellers, I've been following the well-worn path laid out by my guidebook. Conscientiously seeking out all the recommended places to visit, spending a brief while there, then moving on. I've been travelling on autopilot. That's why I've come to this ancient Incan capital. It's a "must-see" for any self-respecting backpacker. Plus, my old friend Avi from my hometown of Walsall currently lives here. I know I should be excited to be here in these idyllic surroundings and eager to see one of my dearest friend. Yet, no matter how hard I try to convince myself that everything is okay, I just don't buy it. For as long as I can remember, I've had a vague, gnawing feeling that something is missing. I don't know what it is or where to look. All I know is I must find it.

A few months ago this desire compelled me to quit my well-paid job and give up my stress-free life in the UK to explore Latin America. I have absolutely no idea what drew me specifically to Latin America other than a realisation I had in meditation class that this was the place I had to visit next.

I sluggishly set off on foot for my accommodation, too tight to pay the S/. 8 (£1.50 / $3) taxi fare. I fail to take into account that the journey is all uphill, and Cusco sits at an altitude of 3300m. Forty-five minutes later, I arrive at the hostel with a banging headache and on the verge of passing out.

Once I've recovered, I go in search of Avi. Walking down the steep, narrow, cobbled streets of the city is like stepping back in time. I can easily imagine these passageways full of the Incas who constructed them.

Everywhere I look is breath-taking stonework—enormous rocks carved into irregular but precise shapes, interlocking perfectly without the need for mortar. Stones hundreds of years old appear to have been laid only yesterday and have survived numerous earthquakes which flattened plenty of the more modern structures. How the Incas moved such enormous stonework, given the tools of the day, is a mystery that has confounded people for centuries.

A barefooted little girl, no more than six years old, tugs on my arm, bringing me back to the present. Wearing a torn, dirty T-shirt and skirt, she tries to sell me sweets and cigarettes from a small tray held in place by a strap around her neck. Although I've seen such poverty all over Latin America, it's always unsettling.

I abruptly pry myself loose from her grasp and cross the Plaza de Armas, Cusco's picturesque main square, then climb the well-worn steps to O'Flaherty's Irish Pub. There, standing behind the bar, I see Avi complete with his customary Mohican haircut. My mood lifts instantly. A wide cheesy grin breaks across his youthful face.

"'Allo mate, fancy seeing you here," I say, trying to sound casual but unable to contain my enthusiasm. He greets me with a heartfelt hug.

The afternoon turns into evening as we catch up on gossip. The bar slowly fills with gringos keen to relate tales of the Inca Trail and Machu Picchu, the well-preserved mountaintop Incan city and tourist Mecca. O'Flaherty's is the meeting place of choice for the weary traveller eager to make up for the four alcohol-free days it takes to walk the Inca Trail. All it takes is a bottle or three of the local Cusqueña beer to make the place more boisterous. Avi keeps my glass topped at all times. It's only on standing to visit the toilet that I'm reminded of the effects of drinking at such high altitude. It takes real concentration to safely negotiate the maze of tables, many now full of disgruntled England football fans lamenting another dismal performance. Incomprehension at the selection of David 'Calamity' James is the topic of conversation at every other table.

It's like I'm back in London, my surroundings virtually indistinguishable from Finnegan's Wake in Ealing where many friends would be sitting at this moment, having identical conversations. I can't decide whether this is comforting or a reminder of why I left.

These carefree travellers are all making the most of their experience here, enjoying the many splendid experiences that this vast continent has to offer. I can hardly look them in the eye. Despondency follows me everywhere I go, coming closer and closer with each encounter.

* * *

Over the next few weeks Avi and I spend hours together at his workplace, flat or in Pi, a quaint little backstreet coffee shop in the San Blas district of town where his girlfriend Eibhlin also makes and sells her own clothes.

With only a few hundred pounds in his pocket and having known Eibhlin for just a week, Avi followed her to Mexico. From there they made their way to Cusco where they've been living for eighteen months. Most people, including me, would consider what he did irresponsible and foolish. However, Avi had total faith that everything would be all right. He said that when he saw an outrageously cheap charter flight to Cancún he took it as a sign that he should join Eibhlin in Mexico. Two weeks later, he was on the plane, having ended a five-year relationship to be with her. Other friends have also talked of signs and synchronicities before, and I've always dismissed them as a romanticised, unrealistic way of viewing the world.

As much as he confounds me, I love being around Avi. He is one of the nicest people I've ever met; always ready with a kind word or gesture for friend or stranger alike. Highly intelligent and capable of succeeding in the conventional career-oriented life, he's perfectly content to roll along, getting whatever work is available when he needs to. Clearly, he knows something that I don't. I want to discover his secret to living effortlessly. Perhaps it's his spirituality. He practises Reiki and meditation and talks about energy and spirits in a way that is very real to him. I know he'd never lie to me. Even so, I find it impossible to believe in such things. In fact, I think the idea of energy is a load of old hippie bullshit. I did practise meditation for a couple of years and certainly found some short-term benefits. However, the brief moments of peace and calm that I experienced in that rarefied environment have never been something I could bring with me into everyday life.

"Have you ever heard of ayahuasca?" Avi asks one afternoon as we sit watching the tourists browse the shops on Carmen Alto, San Blas's High Street.

My heart leaps at the mention of this word. My friend has my full attention. I'm eager for a first-hand account of this mysterious substance. All I've heard is that it can put you in touch with the spirit world. I want so badly to believe there is more to this world than meets the eye. I need something more to bring meaning to my life. Despite my scepticism something draws me toward ayahuasca.

"Yeah, I have mate," I reply excitedly. "Please, tell me all about it."

"Since we came to Cusco, Me and Eibh have drunk it a few times with our Spanish friend Albert. Ayahuasca's a traditional medicine that comes from the Amazon jungle. They've been using it for thousands of years to heal all kinds of illnesses," he explains savouring a sip of his extra-large cappuccino. "This may sound kinda crazy to you, but the ayahuasca's got medicine spirits that come into your body to heal you when you drink." A smile widens across Avi's face, flushed with enthusiasm, "The spirits can fix physical and emotional problems. It usually happens through purging: throwing up or diarrhoea."

"Okay, and what's the fun part? Is it anything like taking acid?" I ask him.

"Not really, no. Superficially it could seem like it because the visuals can be similar. For me, the big difference is that ayahuasca goes much deeper—you work with the spirits to release negativity. It's not like I'm just tripping out." Avi leans in closer, "Last ceremony, Eibh had a really powerful experience. She's got polycystic ovaries and barely ever menstruated as a result. She was in terrible pain in that area for the whole ceremony, like four hours or more. All doubled up and vomiting, she said she felt like she was having an operation. Even though it was brutal, somehow she also felt blissful and safe. And her periods have been regular ever since."

As Avi relates the story, the passion in his eyes captivates me. At the same time, I can't help but remain dubious. What he's saying sounds way too good to be true. I must remind myself again that this is Avi, my friend I've known for fifteen years. Why would he lie or even exaggerate, especially about something as significant as this? A tingling sensation runs up and down my spine as the possibility of this being true awakens a profound desire. And a new feeling—hope.

"Crazy, no?" he concludes and reaches for his coffee. My thoughts turn to my eczema. If the ayahuasca could heal Eibhlin, then maybe it could cure my problem. As a young child large patches of my body were affected by dry, flaky and sore skin, but as I grew older it lessened. By my teenage years, it only appeared occasionally on my neck, the insides of my elbows or the backs of my knees. A little steroid cream would soon get rid of it. In the last few years, however, it started getting worse. For the first time, it appeared on my feet then spread to other areas of my legs. The cream still suppressed it, but the eczema began to recur more and more frequently. Soon, it began to appear on my back, arms and face.

Now, a full break out can come on at a moment's notice, especially after drinking alcohol. Now, it never goes away completely. On more than one occasion during this trip it got so bad that I almost returned to England.

Since being in Cusco I've noticed something very curious about this condition: whenever I scratch, a sensation runs down inside my body from the point of contact all the way to my left leg and into my foot, which then twitches uncontrollably. It's an uncomfortable feeling and a very strange one at that, almost as if something inside my left foot is causing the eczema.

Although I'd never admit it to anyone else, and have trouble accepting it myself, I also have deep emotional issues that desperately need addressing. I feel severely disconnected from life and other people. Maybe, just maybe, ayahuasca can help me with these problems as well. Without a doubt, I will participate in the next ceremony.

* * *

For the next few weeks, thoughts of ayahuasca surface frequently, as often as the itching of my skin. Eventually, I get Albert's phone number. He'll be holding a ceremony at his house on Saturday night.

When the big day arrives, I'm excited as I am apprehensive.

SHEDDING THE LAYERS

Since I've been told not to eat anything after midday, I head to Jack's cafe in town for a huge English breakfast, as much to calm my emotions as fill my belly.

I spend the afternoon trying to relax, the nervousness increasing as the hours tick slowly by. Excitement and fear battle for supremacy until 8 p.m. finally arrives when two friends and I leave for Albert's on the outskirts of Cusco.

His wife shows us inside. The house is modern and tidy. Stacks of natural history documentaries and children's DVDs fill the bookshelves. I could easily be in any family home back in Britain. The only difference being that in preparation for the ceremony, the living room has been cleared of its sofas and table. In their place, cushions are lined side-by-side along the walls.

"*Bienvenidos,*" comes a friendly, soft-spoken voice from the doorway. "*Siéntense.*"

About fifty years old with a well-groomed beard, flecked with grey, Albert welcomes us with a disarming smile and invites us to take a seat. We choose our places, each of us clutching blankets, as we heard that ayahuasca can make you extremely cold.

Albert's presence is so peaceful that I'm immediately put at ease. I know he's the right person to drink ayahuasca with for the first time. I relax further as I watch one of his young daughters skip around the house as if all the strangers sitting on her living room were family.

"How are you feeling?" I ask Erik, the thirty-year-old Swiss guy who's staying at the same guesthouse as me and is always keen to try something new.

"Excellent," he replies, with no sign of trepidation. "Ready for action."

The third member of our group is Siobhan. She's in her late twenties, slim and attractive with long dark hair. Like most Irish girls who spend more than a few weeks in this town, she works at O'Flaherty's. When not pulling pints she can usually be found propping up the other side of the bar, maintaining her nation's reputation for drinking prowess. Siobhan is also Erik's girl of the week. She joined us on a whim, having only found out what we were up to a few hours ago.

"I'm terrified," she says. "I'm not sure I want to do this after all."

"Everything's going to be just fine," I say, as much to reassure myself as her. "We're in very good hands."

Siobhan's eyes flick up at mine, then return to her finger nails which she's been biting. As apprehensive as she may be she isn't going to back out now.

The doorbell rings. We're joined by a couple of locals who smile sheepishly and quietly settle onto cushions beside us. Albert returns a few minutes later with a large glass bottle; a brown, muddy liquid sloshes around inside.

My heart pounds faster with each glass being filled. Willing myself to calm down, I breathe long and slowly. Albert comes to me and smiles broadly as he pours the murky liquid into my glass. To a chorus of "salud" we all drink. The ayahuasca is bitter and the consistency of blood. My stomach recoils as I gulp it down.

Albert puts on some New Age-style music and lights incense, its sweet smell transports me to the Buddhist centre I used to visit. After a minute or so, Albert extinguishes the candles, plunging us into total darkness.

About twenty minutes later, I begin to feel a heaviness in my body, as though a huge weight is crushing me, forcing me to lie down. Waves of nauseating dizziness cascade through me as kaleidoscopic patterns come swirling into view. I try to fight the rising panic by opening my eyes, but the shapes remain, superimposed on the outlines of the living room. Now I'm trapped halfway between worlds.

Suddenly, I'm aware of Siobhan next to me crying, "It's so horrible! Make it stop. Make it stop," she repeats, then abruptly gets up and dashes out of the room. Albert's wife follows her.

The nausea continues unabated for hours. I'm convinced that vomiting will relieve me of the discomfort yet no matter how hard I try, I can't. The multi-coloured shapes persist, dancing in time to the music. As they bob and weave round the room, my eyes strain to keep up with them for more than a second.

Sensing my distress, Albert comes over to me and places a few drops of flowered water on the top of my head. With all of my senses heightened, its pleasing aroma fills my being, instantly clearing the nausea and saturating me with lightness and beauty.

Wow, I am a child of God. I really do have a soul.

Where did those thoughts come from? I certainly don't believe in God. Yet the unearthly sensations in my body speak of a higher power, of something otherworldly and magnificent.

All night long, I have the feeling that if I could just throw up I would heal my eczema. Eventually, I resign myself to the fact that it's not going to happen tonight. I must be patient. After four arduous hours, I'm finally able to sit up, back to a normal state of awareness.

I turn to Siobhan who was finally persuaded to return to her seat. "How are you doing?" I ask. Even though she has stopped crying, her brow is deeply furrowed and her nails bitten down to the quick.

"That was one of the worst experiences of my life," she replies. "All I could feel was total sadness, like that's all that existed and all that would ever exist in the world. I didn't think it was ever going to stop. I am never, ever doing this again."

Erik, on the other hand, smiles serenely and breathes deeply as if savouring his memories of the experience. "I had such a beautiful time," he tells us. "I could actually feel energy running through my body. I was able to play with it. You know, move and shape it in my hands."

Despite the experience not being as profound as I was hoping for, the vague sense of the divine leads me to believe that there could be some truth to the healing properties of ayahuasca. Deep down I feel certain—beyond anything my rational mind can comprehend—that there is something going on that I can't grasp. I will drink again.

* * *

A few days later, I take a bus out to Pisac, a picturesque town in the Sacred Valley outside of Cusco. While wandering through its famous market, I come across a poster for an ayahuasca retreat centre near the jungle town of Puerto Maldonado, not too far away. It offers a week's stay at a jungle lodge, together with a program of meditation and three ayahuasca ceremonies. I had no idea such places existed.

My instincts tell me that this is of vital importance to my life—an opportunity to drink the sacred brew in its traditional jungle setting; so much more fitting than in the living room of a suburban house. There's nothing I want or need to do more during the rest of my stay in South America.

On my return to Cusco, I get online right away to book the trip. Instead, I find myself searching for other organisations running similar workshops. When I come across the website for a company called Blue Morpho, I feel as though I've been struck by a thunderbolt. *This is it, this is it* screams a voice in my head. For a moment, I feel so dizzy I think I might pass out.

Then, my mind becomes silent. There isn't the usual flood of "yeah buts" and "what ifs". There's just a quiet knowing. As illogical as the decision may be, I trust it.

I have found the next step on my journey.

CHAPTER 2
Into the Other World

As much as my mind wanders in flights of fancy about what the coming week might have in store for me, the soreness of my skin pulls me back. I walk down the steps onto the tarmac at Iquitos airport. Despite only being 8 a.m., the wall of heat and humidity that hits me suggests that I will be in for a period of intense discomfort.

My curiosity about what's to come lingers with me as I check in to a city centre hotel and go for a short wander around town. The tireless buzz of more than 20,000 moto-taxis swarms around me like mechanical mosquitoes. What strikes me most about the place is the lack of cars—ninety-nine percent of the traffic is moto-taxis, motorbikes and the occasional bus. The sight of entire families balanced precariously on a tiny motorbike, wearing t-shirts, shorts, flip-flops and no helmets is commonplace.

The largest city in the world with no road links, the only way in or out of Iquitos is by boat or plane. Iquitos grew into an important centre in the late nineteenth century due to the Rubber Boom. Today, it has a population of around 400,000 and as the number one destination for those wishing to visit this part of the Amazon jungle, sustains itself in large part through tourism. Safe and friendly, it's a perfect place to spend a day or two after returning to civilization. There's little to keep the traveller here longer.

Later, I meet Hamilton, the owner of Blue Morpho, who also happens to be the tour guide, boat driver, translator and master shaman. 6' 3" tall, blond-haired, blue-eyed, complete with classic American good looks, one would expect Hamilton to be surfing his native Californian coastline rather than living and working among the natives of the Amazon. He greets me with a firm handshake and a friendly grin. As we exchange pleasantries, he looks me directly in the eye with a kind, penetrating gaze. He, along with two other intrepid explorers and I, will be travelling deep into the rainforest and even deeper into our own inner landscapes.

Together we savour our final meal in relative civilisation. JC, a huge, jovial man of around forty, is an IT director of a venture capital firm. He has worked with Native American shamans near his Californian home. The other guest is Brandon. Also from the US, he's a teacher in his mid-twenties with unruly, thick black hair and a rough-hewn beard to match. Friendly and engaging, he gives off the impression of the hippie-type that I'd expected to find around ayahuasca.

Hamilton soon starts to tell us about how, at twenty-six years of age, he came to be living in the middle of the Amazon jungle as a master ayahuasca shaman. As he speaks, I sense a power and an understanding that belie his youth. His soulful blue eyes reflect his profound knowledge of life. It's clear he's had his fair share of tough times.

"After finishing college a few years ago, I reached a crisis point in my life," he begins. "I wasn't suicidal. I'd just had enough, and my biggest fear was having to live my life all the way until I died. One night I had an argument with my mom and ended up blaming her for giving birth to me. Basically, I told her I never asked to be born.

"'Fine,' she said. 'If you don't want your life any more, give it back to Spirit.'"

Hamilton laughs as he recalls that this was the dumbest thing he'd ever heard. His mom became "spiritual" a few years earlier after going through a difficult divorce. He decided the only way he could prove her wrong, that there were no such things as spirits, was to do exactly what she said. So he started screaming at the wall, pleading if there really was anything out there, for it to come and help him.

"There was no flash of lightning, but I had an awesome cathartic experience. I began crying uncontrollably. It was one of the most honest moments of my life. The very next night I had my first encounter with Spirit. As I slept, I had an out-of-body experience. Suddenly, I was completely awake, absolutely not dreaming, and I was taken on a journey to a city in another world where I interacted with various spirits."

It's hard to reconcile the tale that I'm hearing with the person telling it. This is no New-Age, far-out hippie. This is the son of a plastic surgeon, speaking sincerely.

"Later," Hamilton continues, "I found myself back in my bedroom, hovering over my body, before descending back into it. Right then, I saw a light coming down the hall. It was my mom coming into the room. She told me she loved me very much, that everything had been planned by Spirit, and it was all going to be okay. Then she turned and left."

Hamilton goes on to explain how, completely spooked by this, he went to his mom's room to ask her what was going on only to find her fast asleep. He woke her and she told him she was asleep the entire night. That's when the truth hit him—actually it was her spirit that came to him.

"From that day on," he says, looking each of us in the eye in turn, "I've been able to see and interact with spirits in normal waking consciousness every day of my life."

I manage an awkward smile, nod and tentatively say, "Cool."

Hamilton continues to tells about his first interactions with spirits, how they'd settle at the bottom of his bed at night and be there waiting when he woke up; how they'd sit next to him on the sofa and in the backseat of his car. Terrified, he'd insist that it didn't matter if he could see them. He still didn't have to believe they existed.

Some time later, his mom introduced him to a female shaman to help him make sense of what was happening. The shaman told him that he had two options: forget anything ever happened and go back to his old life; or give himself over and find out what it all meant.

Hamilton smiles ruefully, "I got myself into this mess by giving my life back. So it wasn't my decision to make anymore," he explains. "I knew I had to walk this path to the end, wherever it would lead."

Learning quickly how to put himself into trance, he made shamanic journeys every night to visit his spirit guides who would help him release fear and past emotional hurts. One night, they told him that he would go to Peru where a shamanic apprenticeship awaited him, and he would soon become a master shaman.

"You guys are crazy," he told them. "I'm going to Brazil to finish working on my novel. Besides, I can't afford to go to both Peru and Brazil."

Every night, however, they told him the same thing and even gave him a specific website where they said he'd find a half-price ticket to Peru valid for ninety days—enough time for him to find his apprenticeship.

"What could I do?" he asks, chuckling. "I checked out the website and all the flights were like eight or nine-hundred bucks. Then, on the third or fourth night, sure enough there it was: a return ticket from San Francisco to Lima for four hundred bucks, good for exactly ninety days."

Still not entirely convinced, he asked his mom for advice. She told him he had to buy the ticket. So on September 10, 2001, he was on a plane to Lima.

"I was totally petrified," he admits. "Just a few months ago I didn't believe in spirits, and then there I was on my way to Peru in search of a prophetical apprenticeship. Sure, it was crazy. But it was also super exciting."

Every night while in Peru he would do a journey to contact his spirit guides who would tell him where to go next. After some time travelling around, Hamilton found himself in the Amazon where a guide took him to a remote part of the jungle, an entire day by boat from Iquitos—to a place that would become the location of the Blue Morpho camp.

There, he met a local shaman and participated in his first ayahuasca ceremony. Hamilton describes it as "the most terrifying, most beautiful, darkest, lightest, saddest and most joyous experience of my life."

"It was," he says, "everything."

He didn't realise that he'd been given a massive dose of ayahuasca, the guide having told the shaman to "blow the gringo's socks off."

"After a few minutes it became so intense that I thought, *If this doesn't get any stronger I'll be okay*," Hamilton recalls. "In fact, it got consistently stronger for the next four hours. There were hummingbirds with fifty-foot wingspans all around me, and the bush next to me had turned into a wild boar that was screaming obscenities at me, telling me what a bad job I was doing at managing my ceremonial experience. Then I became convinced I was dying."

Since he hadn't died after hours of abject terror, Hamilton eventually stopped resisting the experience.

"All of a sudden I was presented with two gateways. The one on the left was full of light and love and divinity. The one on the right was a vortex of total insanity. 'Choose!' a booming voice said, and I thought *I'm going left*. Well you would, right? Unfortunately, when I tried to enter I hit an invisible barrier. I tried a second time and the same thing happened. On the third attempt, the gateway disappeared, leaving this vortex of insanity that started sucking me in. I totally panicked. I knew with complete certainty that if I went down there I wouldn't be okay. No doubt, I would be spending the rest of my life in an asylum."

All three of us listen transfixed.

"Right then the same voice roared at me, 'Work!' and I was confronted with everything that was negative from my past—every lie I'd told, every time I'd gotten angry, every time I'd hurt somebody. It was pain, suffering, trauma, sadness. Imagine thirty strobe lights going off simultaneously with every flash a negative thought or action from the past. I had to apologise, forgive and release all that energy. Whenever the intensity got too much, and I couldn't release it fast enough, I'd vomit and get about three seconds' break to breathe before another wave hit."

And so it went for a couple of hours until Hamilton felt like he couldn't go on. He was face down in the dirt with just enough energy to move his head six inches to the side to throw up so he wouldn't be lying in his own vomit. Even if the ayahuasca wasn't going to kill him, he thought he might well die from exhaustion. That's when the shaman, who had been silently watching all this time, came over and blew tobacco smoke on his chest.

Hamilton continues, "Immediately, I felt a contraction in my stomach like nothing I'd felt before. The pain was excruciating. A heavy object started moving slowly up into my throat as a force crushed my esophagus from underneath, like it was trying to prevent the object from falling down into my stomach. Finally, I vomited this nasty ball of dense liquid that was the size of a lemon. It was like neon green, molten metal.

"Suddenly, the vortex of insanity was gone, and the gateway to divinity reappeared. Rather than having to go through, it came and surrounded me. Inside were all my spirit guides, ancestors, friends, family and every person I ever met in my life. There were millions of spirits, all clapping and cheering, saying, 'We knew you could do it. Congratulations, you've found your apprenticeship.'

"*You've got to be kidding!* I thought," Hamilton says, concluding his story.

As we go on to chat into the early hours of the morning, I'm seriously debating about what I've gotten myself into. A part of me really wants to believe all this madness. But my dominant rationality kicks back in and reminds me that this has to be pure fantasy.

Then, Hamilton tells us he's been simultaneously holding a number of conversations with different spirits. My eyes dart around the room, searching for something out of the ordinary. My lips curl up into a smile.

"I'd really love to believe you," I tell him, "but this all sounds too crazy."

"That's okay," he replies. "You have a very narrow view of reality. We'll do something about that this week."

As I walk back to the hotel, head spinning with thoughts of spirits, I wonder whether I will get to encounter them over the coming days. Frankly, what Hamilton has told me is off the fucking wall.

Despite all my disbelief and trepidation, something deep inside reassures me that I'm in the right place. This is where I'm meant to be. I'm determined to find out what, if any of this, is true.

* * *

The next afternoon, we board the dilapidated three-storey metal contraption that will take us on a fourteen-hour journey up the Amazon. I watch as hundreds of locals rush to find hanging space for their hammocks on deck. Fifteen minutes of chaos and tangled rope ensue as hammocks are strung side by side and on top of each other, leaving no more than an inch or two of breathing space between. Fortunately, we have our own cabins. They may only consist of two narrow wooden benches, one above the other, but at least we'll have some privacy and a place to lock our belongings. As the boat makes its way slowly out of the city, the sun slips into the river. A burnished orange spreads across the sky, its glow shimmering like a thousand fish swimming just below the water's surface.

As we dine on a traditional meal of chicken and plantains, Hamilton introduces us to the concepts behind the way ayahuasca works, "At the most fundamental level everything in the Universe is made up of energy. When you drink ayahuasca you take the spirits of the plants into your body where they'll travel all around, seeking out and removing 'crossed energy', which can manifest as physical illness, past mental or emotional traumas, or spiritual ailments. At this level of working there's no differentiation. It's all energy that no longer serves you. It's got to come out. So you ask the spirits to heal it. Then, sit back and let them do their job."

Sorry Hamilton. Sounds too easy and too good to be true.

After the break of dawn we arrive at the village of Jenaro Herrera, where we disembark and go in search of breakfast. Dogs laze contentedly in the middle of the dusty main street. Children chase footballs, squealing in delight, while the adults smoke silently in rocking chairs. The pace of life here is slow, even compared to the laid-back attitude of Iquitos.

While we're enjoying our breakfast, Hamilton is out getting the next leg of the journey prepared. After registering our whereabouts with the local police, we're back on the river. Hamilton steers one of his thirty-foot dugout canoes. A local guide is in charge of the other. It's filled with the food, drink and other supplies we'll need during our stay since the nearest store with the most basic goods is back in Herrera, a three-hour ride from camp.

We travel up the Ucayali River, a tributary of the Amazon,

crossing the Supay lagoon where we catch a glimpse of the famous, pink river dolphin cavorting playfully in the distance. From there, it's on to Blue Morpho on the banks of the Aucayacu River. Along the way, we pass single-storey wooden houses and children washing clothes at the river's edge, waving cautiously at the canoe of passing white men. As the gentle progress of the boat carries us further into the jungle, a force pulls me deeper into myself, into my fears. *What if what Hamilton says is true, and I have to directly face my demons? Will I be strong enough to conquer them?*

By early afternoon, the boats pull up in front of the camp—the last house in the last community on this stretch of river. From here, you would have to travel six days overland to find the nearest upriver inhabitants: native tribes living on the Peruvian-Brazilian border. We enter the main building, known as the long house. It is fully screened, a real luxury around here. Though far from perfect the screens manage to deny entry to the majority of winged beasts, which is just as well since outside the mosquitoes are thick and fierce.

As we wait for the boats to be unloaded, we relax in rocking chairs that ring a small table in the centre of the room. A couple of hammocks swing in the breeze behind us. This main room doubles as the ceremonial space and will be cleared at night. Situated nearest the door are a dining table and two benches. Mosquito nets are strung at the far end of the room that leads to a bathroom area with a river-water shower, toilet and sink.

Brandon and I are based in the camp's other building—a small bungalow located fifty yards up a gently inclining path, lined with flowering shrubs and plants. On the way to our accommodation, we pass the outside kitchen where our neighbour, on whose land the camp is built, will be preparing all our meals. Our bungalow contains two thin mattresses, each covered by a mosquito net, and a bathroom, similar to the one in the long house.

Hamilton and JC will sleep in the long house, along with the final member of our party, Alberto Torres Dávila, the other master ayahuasca shaman who will preside over the ceremonies. It was under his guidance that Hamilton completed his apprenticeship. A month ago he was given the title *maestro*, meaning master shaman, the highest rank in their lineage—a process which usually takes between five and ten years. Hamilton, however, completed his apprenticeship in under two years.

The contrast between the two maestros could not be more striking. More than a foot shorter than Hamilton, Alberto is in his late forties with dark, greying hair, permanently hidden under a baseball cap. At first, shy and quiet in the presence of us gringos, this slight man is considered one of the most powerful and revered healers in this part of the jungle. Hamilton shares a joke with him. Alberto's laughter is infectious. We can't help but laugh along even though we've no idea what they're talking about.

Alberto came to shamanism at eight years old when his grandfather, also an *ayahuasquero*, gave him tobacco juice to drink.

"To stop me from growing up lazy," he tells us in his jungle-Spanish dialect. He first drank ayahuasca a year later and soon decided that he wanted to learn this ancient medicine, passed down in his family for many generations. By the age of fourteen, Alberto was going off into the jungle alone for weeks at a time to diet the medicinal plants.

According to Hamilton, one can only become a master shaman through shamanic diets that involve drinking a tea made from the barks of medicinal trees. Doing so invites the spirits of the particular trees to live inside your body where they help remove crossed energy and teach you how to become a healer.

In a canoe that he built himself, Alberto would travel three or four days away from his home where he'd construct a basic shelter and catch fish. He would also hunt animals, smoke the meat and take it home with him as payment for his apprenticeship. By seventeen, he was considered a master shaman and started working as a healer. At this time, he also met his partner with whom he has eight children. For the last thirty years, Alberto has continued his shamanic work, recently forming a pact with Hamilton that they will work together until death.

With this unlikely couple, we venture out the following morning, watching them harvest the ayahuasca vine and a number of tree barks that are to go into the mixture. The spirits of these plants, Hamilton tells us, will be called into the ceremony to help our healing.

Back at camp, we're each handed a mallet and set to work on smashing the ayahuasca into small pieces—tough, sweaty work given the heat and humidity. The final ingredient is leaves of the chacruna plant, which give the ayahuasca its visionary property. Everything is placed sequentially into a huge pot, which is then filled with river water and left to boil over a wood-burning fire for the rest of the day.

At lunch, we're treated to a local delicacy, *majas*. Being a member of the rodent family, Hamilton jokingly refers to it as "jungle rat." My initial repulsion at the thought of eating rat makes me want to push it slowly around my plate as I used to do with inedible school dinners. However, I figure I'll be doing scarier things this week. I brave a small mouthful.

It's surprisingly tasty and comes with the staple fare of rice and plantain. Our food during the week will be basic—chicken, fish and eggs mostly. This meal will be our last of the day, as several hours of fasting are compulsory on days of ceremony. So, with the heat of the day reaching its peak, there's little option but to head to a hammock for a siesta.

As the sun begins to disappear behind the treetops, the shamans remove the brew from the fire, filtering and straining it through cheesecloth before pouring it into a large glass bottle and placing it on ice to cool. What started out seven hours ago as a forty-litre pot of vines, leaves, bark and water has now been reduced to no more than two litres of thick, brown, bubbling liquid. It's chunkier and darker in colour than the ayahuasca I drank back in Cusco.

A sense of foreboding accompanies me to my mosquito net. I lie waiting for 9 p.m. to arrive while the jungle comes to life. The deafening sounds of the insects heighten my apprehension. I'm terrified yet determined. I've come a long way to do this. The trust I have in Hamilton and Alberto, and for the brew itself, goes beyond any rational sense. If there is an unknown part of myself, a soul or spirit or whatever, then the ayahuasca is speaking to it now, for my conscious awareness is telling me the wisest course of action is to run as far away from here as possible.

Despite the nearly unbearable muggy weather, I put on a long-sleeve shirt and long trousers in an attempt to avoid mosquito attack as I walk to the long house. Transformed since the afternoon, it's bare of table, chairs and hammocks. In their place, three mattresses lie on the wood-slatted floor. Beside each is a cup of water, toilet paper and plastic bowl (lovingly referred to as a "puke bucket"). In front of the mattresses are two rocking chairs surrounded by numerous bottles of exotic potions. Seated in those chairs calmly smoking *mapacho*, jungle tobacco that bears more of a resemblance to cigars than cigarettes, are the two men in whose hands we're about to trust our lives. As if it were any other evening spent among good friends, Alberto and Hamilton joke together in the jungle dialect that my reasonable amount of Spanish cannot decipher.

Two kerosene lamps give off a golden, smoky glow, heightening the eerie atmosphere and the electric tension in the air. I choose the mattress on the far right. I smile nervously at Hamilton who chuckles like an expectant child. He gives us a final few words of advice:

"Focus on positive thoughts, relax and let go of all expectations. If it gets tough, just laugh and be thankful."

Sure…

The shamans cover their bodies with the various bottled mixtures, Hamilton explaining each contains a different plant to protect their bodies spiritually. One of these is camalonga, a plant that teaches through one's dreams. Another is "vampire juice" a mixture of male garlic and camphor in a sugarcane liquor.

"Hollywood got that part right," Hamilton tells us, smiling as he rubs it on his arms and on top of his head. "They really don't like garlic."

Turning to Alberto on his left he asks, "*¿Listo maestro? ¿Le doy?*" Are you ready, maestro? Shall I begin? It's as though my whole life has been in preparation for this moment.

The three of us watch intently as Hamilton blows smoke from his mapacho into the bottle of ayahuasca, then sings *icaros* into it. Although they sound like songs, they are in fact commands to the medicine spirits, taught during apprenticeship by the spirits themselves. Alberto follows suit, adding his own force and energy to the brew.

Before I know it, I'm holding a small metal cup. My scepticism will not allow me to believe that this thick brown sludge actually contains spirits willing to help me heal physically and emotionally. But, on the off chance that they do exist and can hear my thoughts, I tell them how scared I am and ask them to be gentle with me. Searching for a space free of thought, free of doubt, I down the concoction in one gulp.

Once everybody, including the shamans, has drunk, the kerosene lamps are extinguished. The shrill calls of the crickets and frogs in the distance intensify as we sink into darkness so thick I can't tell if my eyes are open or closed.

It's not long before the hypnotic beat of the *shacapas*, the leaf rattles used by the shamans to direct and move energy, coupled with the enchanting sounds of the icaros, send me into a trance. As I drift away, my body is compressed into the mattress, as though an elephant were sitting on my chest.

In the blink of an eye, I find myself flying through a technicolor landscape of geometric patterns; structures that change so quickly in time with the icaros that my mind cannot keep pace. Disorientating and nauseating, it's a thousand times more intense than the most sickening fairground ride.

Extreme physical exhaustion hits me like a sledgehammer, accompanied by a barrage of self-negating thoughts. Certain that I don't have the strength to deal with them I try desperately to push them away. Then I feel Hamilton's presence as if he were standing right next to me. Boundaries dissolve as streams of energy flow between us at the speed of light. *Get out of my mind!* I want to shout. *Stop reading my thoughts.* Huge waves of panic wash over me, along with the shame of somebody knowing my deepest fears.

I'm fighting an impossible battle: destructive ideas that I've held about myself and buried deep in my unconscious for many years are now being prised loose by the medicine. As they pass through my consciousness, I feel the pain of decades of self-loathing. As if that isn't enough, all my beliefs about life are being shattered. My mind tries desperately to piece its old reality back together.

All night long the intense itching of my skin suggests that ayahuasca is working on my physical body too. In search of relief I dig my nails into my tender flesh, sending lightning bolts of electricity through my body, directly into my left foot, which shakes violently and throbs. Once whatever has caused this is removed I'm sure the illness and suffering will be gone from my body as well.

After a period of time that could've been anything from an hour to a week the hut gradually comes back into focus. The ceremony has come to an end. While Hamilton and Alberto congratulate each other on a job well done, my mind continues to reel, frenziedly trying to comprehend what has just happened. All I can be sure of is one thing—everything that happened was absolutely real, not simply a drug "trip". It's impossible to articulate or explain to myself how they differ. It's just a knowing, beyond any words or explanation.

"Sleep well," Hamilton says to us. "Tomorrow we do it all again."

Morning arrives all too soon. My head and body complain vigorously at my attempts to get out of bed. An early morning dip in the river succeeds in removing the lingering effects of the ayahuasca. After five minutes I feel revived and awake, ready for breakfast. While we eat Hamilton tells us that right where we were swimming they found a six-metre long anaconda last week. I make a mental note to stick to the shower in future.

I listen to JC and Brandon discuss last night's blissful experiences and their interactions with beings of light. How desperately I want to believe in the wonder and the goodness of life. All the people that I've met who were, for want of a better term, "spiritual", seem so much happier and more peaceful than the rest of society, myself especially.

My experience the previous evening confirms that there is indeed something else out there. Whether or not I like it is still very much in the balance.

* * *

SHEDDING THE LAYERS

It stirs inside me, and I start to writhe on the mat, fighting desperately to gain control over my body. Soon I'm kicking my legs and flailing my arms, thrashing on the unyielding floor and screaming at the top of my lungs: "Get it out of me, get it out of me, I don't want it anymore! Help me, help me!"

Then the mattress disappears. No more house. No more icaros. No more ceremony. Only complete and utter chaos and terror. Unable to process a thought, I spiral through a web of madness.

There is a sound, a voice, somewhere nearby. It's telling me to calm down, that everything is okay. Hamilton is by my side, reminding me that I'm in an ayahuasca ceremony. *Now I remember. Okay, breathe, focus, this is a good thing Mark. You're purging negative energies.* I relax, aware momentarily of my surroundings, but the dark spirit is not done with me. From a prone position I suddenly flip up onto the top of my head—without using my arms or legs. I hold the inverted pose like a freeze-frame break-dancer, balancing in mid-air for several seconds, before somebody pulls me back down onto the mattress.

Hamilton tries to grab hold of my legs. I manage one good solid kick to his head before he pins me to the ground. The two helpers, Pedro and Rosa, have an arm each. Between them they make sure I can't do myself or anyone else more damage.

When it becomes clear that I'm not going to respond to words, Hamilton picks me up and half-carries, half-drags me to the shower, continuing to restrain me in a bear hug as the water rains down on our clothed bodies. Eventually, I begin to calm down and return to my body. Hamilton sits me on the floor outside of the shower and tells me to focus on light and love, to go into my heart.

My heart! The mere mention of the word conjures forth visions of demonic entities, spitting fire and tormenting me mercilessly. "You are worthless. You don't deserve to be happy. You are incapable of experiencing love," they scream.

I am never, ever, EVER doing this again, I say to myself as I search for a way out, for a glimmer of light, the slightest glimpse of hope. *At this point, death would be a welcome alternative.*

As the power of fear and hatred threatens to drive me back over the edge, I desperately attempt to focus. The harder I try, the faster my head vibrates until something cracks, followed by a rushing sound. I vomit again and again. The stench of death fills the air.

Seconds later, the purest peace I've ever felt fills my body. Like a newborn I open my eyes and see the world for the first time, as it really is: pristine, beautiful and perfect—from the lady sitting opposite me, to the floorboards and the harmonious way they fit together, to the floral pattern on the shower curtain.

Wait a minute, who's that lady?

Turning to look at her again she appears to be about forty years old. With long, flowing white hair and a serene, blissful expression, she radiates love and grace. Her green-eyed gaze transfixes me.

"I'm your Guardian Angel," the sparkling, emerald pools that are her eyes announce. My heart bursts open. Joy and gratitude spill out. I'm awash with tranquillity. This interaction is perfectly normal. I beam a big smile in her direction. No longer can I doubt the existence of spirits. I revel in this heavenly bliss until I remember that my clothes are soaking wet.

"Good work," Hamilton shouts to me as I re-enter the main part of the house in a dry set of clothes. "I think we scored a ten on the intensity scale tonight!"

"What on earth happened?" I ask him.

"Well, while you were thrashing around there was an enormous black demon coming out of you," he says matter-of-factly. "It stretched up about thirty feet, right to the roof of the building. That thing was

SHEDDING THE LAYERS

mean, and it didn't want to come out. But we got him. That's the first time I've had to put someone in the shower. Congratulations!"

I'm not sure this is something to be proud of.

* * *

The gentle splash of the paddles on the water and the occasional bird call are the only sounds as the canoe drifts lazily along the Aucayacu River. On either side, the massive walls of jungle foliage make it virtually impossible to spot wildlife. Fortunately, I'm with an expert. Hernán, our local guide, is attuned to life out here. He effortlessly spots birds and spiders that I would have missed even with binoculars.

As dusk approaches, we rest our paddles, letting the current lead us back towards camp. My skin prickles in the heat and humidity, reminding me of my physical limitations. The gentle power of the water carries me on to the next stage of my journey, filling me with the strength required to heal my body. "You can do it," it whispers to me. "You are stronger than you think."

Hernán brings me out of my reverie. He turns around, puts his finger to his lips in the universal gesture of "be quiet" and brings the canoe to a halt. After staring intently into the jungle for a minute or so, he mouths the word "*monos*" (monkeys), pointing way up high in the trees. I follow his finger to find a family of five tiny spider monkeys leaping one after another from branch to branch. They move with grace and ease, not a care in the world.

On our return to camp, I join the others around the dinner table. Looking at the tall, young American sitting opposite me, I struggle to reconcile Hamilton's outward appearance with his occupation. For me the word "shaman" conjures up exotic images of old native Indian men, naked save for a loin cloth and ceremonial headdress. Bodies covered in bright paint, they dance ecstatically, communicating with unseen beings.

To have moved to this remote area of the world at such a young age and embark on a traditional apprenticeship that very few Westerners have previously undertaken required an unfathomable degree of courage and probably no small amount of recklessness. Having experienced a little of the power of ayahuasca, it's clear that anyone who could manage such a ceremony must have extraordinary abilities.

He speaks in detail about his own spiritual realisations that are on a par with the enlightened masters. He does so in such a down-to-earth way that my own doubts and disbeliefs resurface each time.

If this were all true, shouldn't he be more spiritual, more reverent?

To Hamilton, God is "The Dude". He recounts conversations that they've had together, as well as telling us that Jesus is one of his best friends. In the next moment, he repeats a dirty joke that one of the old women in the community told him last week.

Despite his unstinting friendly nature, he does intimidate and scare me. When I talk to him I feel like he's looking right through me, judging me, seeing what a pathetic man I am compared to him. I'm certain that he knows all my secrets. I resent him for being able to see so easily through the facade that I've carefully constructed. My projection of a happy-go-lucky, carefree guy that I thought I carried off quite well is instantly apparent as a sham to Hamilton.

* * *

In the face of my overwhelming terror at the thought of drinking ayahuasca again, I have to find the courage to do it. Last night in ceremony, Hamilton told me that he'd seen something in my left foot. Tonight, he will be sucking it out.

"Make sure you give your foot a good wash," he demands.

An hour into the ceremony, Hamilton tells me it's time to do the work. I know immediately that the icaro he's singing is calling in the assistance of the medicine spirits. I sense a dozen or more of them surround me. Their features blurry, they're more like an ethereal mist. Yet there's no denying their presence.

I take a succession of deep breaths as Hamilton starts sucking vigorously on my sole. When I feel his mouth connect with my foot and actually enter inside it I become weak and disorientated. Periodically, he coughs and spits into his bucket, dispatching whatever he's just removed. By the time he's done, twenty minutes later, he's ashen and exhausted.

Having accidentally ingested some of the poison, Hamilton must have a *venteada*—essentially a shamanic healing. Usually performed only on guests, the strength of this evil has left even a master shaman in need of assistance. So Alberto must step in. He begins singing icaros while playing a shacapa to straighten Hamilton's energy and remove any negative spirits.

"There was a spirit lodged in there," Hamilton tells me after the ceremony. "It was black and hairy, kind of like a sea urchin, and it had tendrils coming out of it that ran all the way up your leg, across your back and into your neck. That's why it was so hard to get it out. The medicine spirits told me that it came from a time when you took LSD."

LSD! I see the truth of it immediately, like a jigsaw piece slotting into place.

CHAPTER 3
LSD and Witchcraft

SHEDDING THE LAYERS

June 2001

The two-lane paved road running north out of Lusaka, Zambia's chaotic capital, cuts through bare scrubland. The only scenery is the occasional lone figure seated at the side of the road, selling their wares—invariably, little more than a few pieces of fruit.

Ninety minutes later, a large, smiley face on the road announces our arrival. Prash, an old friend from my days at Nottingham University, and I jump out of the minibus, glad to be breathing fresh air again. Of Indian descent, with boyish good looks and boundless energy, he is something of a legend. Despite the mischievous glint in his eye, he's usually harmless. Of course there was the time he tried to steal a full-sized fruit machine from a pub.

We pass a small pink and orange sign that reads, "Solipse Festival." A three-hundred-yard dirt track leads to the entrance gate where we're given a map of the site. What was farmland just a few days ago is now a camping area for thousands.

The blazing mid-afternoon sun gives no indication that we're in the middle of winter. The ground all around is a light brown colour, covered with thin, spindly grass. The slightest gust of wind covers us in a fine, sandy dust. Prash and I set up camp in a flat, shaded area before heading out to find my friend Andy.

We met in Melbourne a year ago when we were both working at the offices of a mining company to save money for backpacking around Australia. Andy's ability to create entertainment wherever he goes almost managed to make our dull job enjoyable. Simply being near his cheeky grin was enough to get me through another fifteen minutes of data entry.

During a particularly slow day, he came and told me that he'd invented a skydiving machine. He asked if I wanted to try it. At first,

I thought I'd misunderstood his thick Scouse accent, but he led me to a corner of the office where two colleagues were holding up a board containing a six-foot by-six-foot aerial photograph of a nickel mine.

Having sat me down in an office chair, he put a small rucksack on my back and wheeled me slowly away from the others, all the way to the far wall. He started spinning me round and round, faster and faster until I felt quite sick.

"Put your arms out like this," he said, stretching his up and out at a forty-five degree angle. Totally disorientated, I did as he requested. He grabbed hold of the back of the chair and pushed me across the office, sprinting as fast as he could while imitating the sound of rushing wind. I hurtled straight at the photograph. Right before I crashed into it, Andy put the brakes on, bringing me to rest with my nose touching the picture.

"What d'ya reckon?" he asked. "Skydiving machine. Pretty cool, huh?"

"Genius," I replied. It was hard to argue.

Almost immediately, Prash and I hear Andy's unmistakably loud, inimitable laughter drifting on the breeze. Together, the three of us walk around the site for two hours, familiarising ourselves with its layout. The campgrounds are located at one end with a meeting point and bathing area in the centre. At the other end, a narrow dirt path leads to the entertainment area. The dance floor, a large flat piece of ground, partly shaded by a giant tree, sprawls in front of the ten-feet high, sixty-feet wide stage with speakers towering on either side and a set of DJ decks off to the left. A six-foot tall neon-green head hangs from scaffolding directly above.

As we pass by, a number of people appear on stage, including the Zambian Minister of Culture, who wishes everyone a great stay in his country and officially kicks off the festival.

With some effort, we manage to resist the cold draught beers being served at the bar and wander down through a cool, wooded area into a small glade. In the clearing stands a spacious tent, open at the sides. Cushions and bean bags are scattered all around inside. Floor-to-ceiling Day-Glo paintings hang from the walls. A small counter serves chai tea and carrot cake while ambient music lazes out of the sound system in the corner. The heavy scent of marijuana fills the air, a group of young men and women relaxing nearby. All of them have fat, unhygienic-looking dreadlocks and bright, tie-dyed or flowery clothing. This place is a haven for hardcore travellers, hippies and crusties. With my regulation short haircut and plain t-shirt and shorts I'm definitely the odd one out this week.

As soon as the sun begins to set, we head quickly back towards the campgrounds. This close to the equator, the transition from day to night is almost instantaneous and out here is accompanied by a rapid drop in temperature that can chill you to the bone in minutes. My teeth are chattering by the time I make it back to my tent. Only once I've donned my thermal top, hoodie, fleece and woolly hat am I ready to venture back outside.

"Look what I've got," says Prash, pulling out a huge bag of weed. "That should do for the week," he says with a laugh. "God, it's so cheap here."

A wide variety of drugs are freely on offer all over the site. With no police presence there's no fear of arrest. And all the muscular local men, acting as security guards, couldn't be less concerned about the sale and consumption of drugs. It's not long before we're in possession of a number of Ecstasy tablets. Without drugs these events hold little appeal. I'm generally apprehensive before taking them, aware that this could be the time they seriously harm me. But I always conclude that the chance is slim enough to make it a risk worth taking.

* * *

At the bar, strangers smile and greet us for no reason other than to be friendly. I instinctively react with suspicion and mistrust. There's no way I'll drop my guard. Not even among these seemingly amiable people.

Laughing, drinking, smoking and chatting merrily, everyone sits in groups, all wrapped up against the bitter cold. As usual, I anxiously await my time of escape.

As the evening wears on, the music gets louder, pumping trance into the cold African night, waking up everyone around. Feet begin to tap, heads nod. Before long, like moths to a light, people are drawn inexorably to the dance floor. Soon it's alive with a throng of bodies weaving in time to the electronic beats, fluorescent face paint and glow-sticks streaming through the darkness. In the distance, a crowd has formed a circle. There's a great cheer as flames erupt from its centre. We move quickly to see two girls swinging chains of fire around their bodies, gyrating and writhing to the beat of the music. As they trace elaborate patterns through the air, their arms move faster and faster until they vanish, leaving only trails of fire and a distinctive "whooshing" sound.

My eyes dart around to see if anyone's watching. I take out a small white pill from my pocket and hurriedly swallow it with a swig of water. Thirty minutes later, waves of heat begin to ripple up and down my body. I feel a tingling in my spine and butterflies in my stomach as the Ecstasy works its way into my bloodstream. The sounds take on a new meaning, a greater intensity, and an uncontrollable force moves my being in time to the thumping beats. Deep bass vibrates the earth beneath my feet.

The rushes of pleasure that the drug induces are exhilarating.

A Cheshire cat-like grin breaks out on my face. All thinking stops as I connect with my environment. *This is what it's all about. This is living.* Around me strangers hug and jump in unison, sharing bottles of water and cigarettes. The dance floor is a rolling sea of happy faces. *Deep down we're all the same. I love each and every one of these people.*

Unfortunately, the chemical also brings with it a heightened level of anxiety: *Are people watching me dance? Do I look like I'm off my face? God this is strong, I hope I'm going to be all right. Drink some water, Mark. Not too much, be careful. Maybe I should go and sit down for a bit.*

Despite the running mental commentary, I persist and party long into the night to acts with names such as Stella Nutella and Zion Train. I dance until well after the effects of the chemicals have worn off and my body pleads for bed.

I wake up dripping in sweat and unable to breathe inside my canvas oven. I drag myself outside and can do nothing save slump back down on the hard ground. My head, muscles, bones and even internal organs ache. This must be what it feels like to be one hundred years old. I curl up into the foetal position and try to sleep, but the gnawing loneliness in the pit of my stomach that the drug comedown produces will not allow it.

* * *

"So, do you fancy taking some acid tonight?" I ask Prash, as we sit eating an overpriced dish of pasta and vegetables, containing surprisingly few vegetables.

I look at the cartoon figure on the tiny square of cardboard held gingerly between my thumb and index finger—a recent purchase from a passing stranger.

"Hmm, I'm not sure," Prash says, showing uncharacteristic caution. "I've had a few rough experiences with that stuff."

"It'll be fine," I tell him, sounding chipper. "We'll just take a little bit, no big deal."

"Oh go on then, if you insist," he replies.

Back at our tents, I carefully cut the two tabs in half, then each half into quarters. Together with Andy, the three of us place a quarter on our tongues, allowing the minute quantity of colourless liquid to be absorbed into our system. Not knowing how strong it might be, we're erring on the side of caution.

After an hour or so, nothing much is happening. I take another quarter, the others choosing to wait awhile. A few minutes later, I feel the weight of the dark night constrict my breathing and wonder whether I should have held off a little longer. As we slowly weave through the crowd to the ambient tent, my legs become difficult to control. Looking down at them through the glare of my head-torch I see that they're now six feet long and as bendy as spaghetti. *That's not good.*

After what seems like days, we make it to our destination where I sink into a giant beanbag, which swallows my body whole, making me lose all sense of it. As I look into Andy and Prash's widely dilated pupils we all burst into a fit of hysterics, giggling like little children.

"I think it's working now," Prash says after we calm down.

The next moment I feel fifty pairs of eyes boring into me, furious at my very existence. *Am I being really loud?* I wonder. *All the people in here hate me*, I realise. And then, like snow giving way under the force of an avalanche, the thoughts come tumbling thick and fast: *They can see me for what I really am, a miserable excuse for a human being—too scared to deal with life, preferring instead to hide away behind mind-altering substances. What a worthless little man. God, I despise myself.* The paranoid diatribe is unrelenting. I stare at the Day-Glo designs dancing on the ceiling as my mind wallows in its well-worn rut of fear and negativity.

Prash is talking to me, telling me to get up. I concentrate on my body, struggling to extricate myself from the beanbag. Outside, under the heightened sensitivity of the drug, the cold air penetrates deep into our bones. Shivering uncontrollably, we walk toward the bar and sit nearby on a log in front of a roaring fire. We're instantly mesmerized by the dancing flames.

My mind clearer and calmer now, I ask the others how they're feeling.

"Okay at the moment," Prash replies. "But that could change any second."

"I feel pretty edgy myself," Andy says. "I think a beer would help calm things down."

Simultaneously, we all look at the bar about twenty yards away, and I know that we're all having the same thought.

"Looks like an awfully long way," I say.

"Yep," they both reply.

Following a further few paralysed minutes, Andy says, "Come on look, there are three stools free up there, let's go. I'm not going on my own."

"Okay, I'll come," I say as the heat starts to become uncomfortable.

"Wait for me," Prash says. "I'm not staying here alone."

After just a few steps, I feel a sharp pain in my left foot. I look down, expecting to see a piece of metal or glass jutting out of my trainer, but there's nothing more than a small trinket made of fine animal hairs. I leave it there and join the others for a delicious, refreshing pint of lager.

By the time I reach the bar, the whole atmosphere has changed.

The darkness comes back thicker now, suffocating me. Now, I can sense the spiritual power of this vast continent, mysterious and enticing, beckoning me into its world. It is at once seductive and terrifying. I can feel the presence of dark entities wanting to feed off my soul, trying to suck the life out of me. A strong urge arises to let out a demonic, blood-curdling yell. I manage to resist, downing half my drink in one go.

I must force myself to concentrate on my breathing. It's only my slow, deep breaths that separate me from the malignant forces until daybreak when the drug mercifully wears off.

CHAPTER 4
A Year in Bed

Ten months later, the eczema appeared on my foot. Then it began slowly spreading throughout my entire body. According to Hamilton, when I stepped on that little trinket in Zambia a spirit entered through the chakra in my foot, which wouldn't have happened if the LSD hadn't blown my energetic body wide open.

"It must have been a talisman of some sort containing witchcraft, but I don't think you were targeted specifically," he assures me. "You were just in the wrong place at the wrong time. That continent has some badass dark magic." He pauses, before adding with a wry grin, "If I can give you one piece of advice, it's this: Don't fuck with Africa, dude."

If what Hamilton says is true, it does kind of make sense that he could've removed something evil from my foot. After all, I no longer feel an electric shock shooting down my leg into my foot when I scratch. Hamilton concludes the final ceremony by blowing tobacco smoke into my foot to help the healing process. As he does so, a cleansing and soothing energy travels up my leg, making it tingle delightfully. And with that, the longest, most challenging week of my life is over.

My eczema is healed. That thought alone sends a wave of relief and gratitude throughout my entire being. It's the new beginning I've always wanted, the start of a whole new life. The future is filled with endless possibilities and they're all positive. Never in my life did I think I'd feel so full of hope. I can't wait for family and friends to see the huge changes in me that have taken and will continue to take place.

I hug Hamilton and Alberto good-bye, my heart full of gratitude for their skill and hard work.

Turning to Hamilton, I say, "Nothing personal mate, but I have no desire to see you again for a very long time."

SHEDDING THE LAYERS

* * *

A week after getting home, I go to Nottingham to catch up with old university friends and celebrate the beginning of a new year—a year full of so much promise—and I'm not going to turn down a few beers.

The evening passes in a blur of bars and empty glasses, eventually coming to an end inside a sleeping bag on somebody's floor. A few hours later, my body awakens me clamouring for attention. I'm covered in eczema from head to toe and barely able to move. My whole body is stiff. Bending my arms and legs is difficult. I smother myself in moisturising cream, followed by a good dose of steroid cream.

Now I'm reminded of Hamilton saying that the illness may have entered my bloodstream and a two-week blood-purifying detox diet could be necessary. No matter how strict the diet may be, it will be well worth the effort to finally clean my body out and move on with my life.

So in mid-January, 2005, I start the detox diet—brown rice, quinoa and lightly steamed vegetables during the day, and first thing in the morning and last thing at night, a fist full of flax seeds and a cup of bentonite clay, supposedly excellent for flushing out the system. If it hadn't been for a week of ayahuasca-drinking I'd hardly be able to choke down the sludgy water.

The two weeks pass. My skin is still red and almost certainly getting more so. I'm also having trouble sleeping. Since getting back from South America a month ago, I haven't been able to fall asleep until around 6 a.m. Hour after hour, I lie staring at the ceiling, not even extreme fatigue allowing me to drift off. Since I don't fall asleep until the early morning, I don't wake up until the afternoon. Being winter in Britain, this means I see about two hours of daylight.

Despite the insomnia and worsening condition of my skin, my

faith that I'll soon be healed holds firm, so I continue the diet. It's not long before an inferno begins raging inside my body. Whenever I make even the slightest movement, a blistering heat boils up to the surface of my skin. I sweat and itch uncontrollably. I scratch for hours until my skin is raw and bloody. At night, my face and neck secrete a fetid, yellowy-brown substance. In the morning, I have to peel myself carefully off the pillow.

Despite the severity of my situation and the fact that mere months ago I would've sought immediate, medical attention from a doctor, my belief in natural healing is strong. During my brief time in the jungle, I discovered that life contains something beyond my perception.

Hamilton talked a little about God. While the thought of some mysterious power greater than me was completely off-putting at first, my belief in this concept is growing every week, without any conscious effort, without knowing what "God" is or even what "God" means.

I used to have faith in Western doctors but now it's clear they can do nothing other than suppress the eczema with creams or tablets. It's simply not a viable long-term option, not for me. And my case is an atypical one to say the least. Most people who suffer from severe eczema have had it all their lives. In all my research I've never come across a case like mine that has come on so suddenly and acutely in adulthood. Which is why I'm convinced there's a root cause, thus, a solution to the problem that I will, I must find.

My sister tells me about a colleague who has an aqua-detox machine, a device that looks just like a foot bath and uses ions in the water to pull out toxins from the body. I pay for a course of treatment. At the first session the water quickly turns brackish. *May it please be the toxins in my bloodstream.* A few days later, I feel better and eagerly await the next treatment. Following three more sessions, it's obvious I'm not getting any better.

After two months of constant pain, a gory, red body and being housebound, my condition gets even worse. Despite all my reservations, I have no choice but to see a skin specialist. I make an emergency appointment to get the requisite referral from a GP.

A large, stern-faced, no-nonsense lady from Africa whose surname is unpronounceable by the Walsall public, Dr. Marjorie is known only by her first name.

"I need you to arrange an appointment with a skin specialist please," I tell her without feeling it necessary to explain why.

"Let me take a look at you," she huffs, offended that I'm not interested in her diagnosis. "Get undressed," she commands tersely.

After a cursory glance over my bloody, inflamed body, she tells me that I need to use steroid cream.

"The cream doesn't work," I say, barely managing not to throttle her. "Whenever I stop using it, the eczema returns even worse. As I'm sure you know, at these high doses it's only meant to be used for a few days at a time. Any longer can cause thinning of the skin. I need something stronger than cream."

"Look, there is nothing else I can give you," she responds, her voice rising in irritation. "Eczema is incurable. All we can do is manage it as best as possible," she concludes, adding her voice to the old refrain that I'm unable to accept. There has to be some medicine that's more effective, and a specialist must be the person who knows.

"I can give you a referral, but the waiting list is three to six months."

"Look at me. Do you seriously think I can wait that long?" I say looking her dead in the eye.

"Well, if you're willing to go private you can see someone tomorrow," she reveals reluctantly, as though it were a well-guarded secret. As it turns out, going private simply means paying to jump the queue. I'll be seeing exactly the same doctor.

Dr. Marjorie makes a quick phone call then announces her major accomplishment: she has managed to get me an emergency slot. I won't have to pay after all. She made one phone call and acts as though she really put herself out and did me an enormous favour. She acts as if I'm wasting her time being here; like she has more important things to be getting on with than dealing with sick people. Regardless, I'm thankful for the help, however begrudgingly it may've been given.

"Now go and see the nurse," she says. "She will bandage you up."

The nurse next door carefully applies bandages soaked in a coal-tar solution to flood my cracked, red hands and arms with moisture. I feel like a mummy as I slowly manoeuvre the car home.

The next day, I pack a bag before leaving to see the dermatologist, certain that she'll admit me into hospital immediately upon seeing the severity of my condition. As I sit for an interminable amount of time in the waiting room, it takes all my will and concentration to not throw myself on the floor and writhe in pain, scratching myself like a crazed animal.

"You're very lucky to be seen at such short notice," the doctor informs me when my turn finally comes. "Get undressed and lie on the bed over there."

She spends a few seconds examining me while I explain how the eczema is getting rapidly worse and how I stopped using the steroid cream, as it's no longer effective.

She delivers her diagnosis, "You need to use the steroid cream again to get the eczema under control."

"Look, I told you it doesn't work anymore," I tell her, trying to keep calm. "There must be something else you can give me."

"Take this prescription and come back in four months," she says curtly.

I try once more to make her listen to me, but it's simply no use. Evidently, in the eyes of Western medicine, I'm just someone out to create trouble, not a sick man, desperate to find relief from his constant suffering. Eyes fixed on my feet, I shuffle out of the consultation room. I don't bother making the follow-up appointment.

Can these doctors not comprehend the fact that there must be an underlying cause? Something so extreme and sudden doesn't happen to the body for no reason. *There is no cure*!? My mind rages at the sheer narrow-mindedness.

Back in my bedroom, I crumple to my knees and pound the wall, eventually curling up into the foetal position. As I lie on the floor, my thoughts return to what I discovered in the Amazon jungle. Ayahuasca medicine operates on an energetic level, where physical, emotional and mental issues are all seen as the same—all of which can contribute to physical illness. This ancient form of healing contains a depth of knowledge unknown to conventional medicine. Perhaps, Western doctors can offer no insight because they cannot see beyond the superficial, physical level.

When the eczema first started to spread a few years ago, I went to an acupuncturist called Laurence, recommended by a friend who had been cured of the same disease. Back then, the treatment caused the eczema to spread across my entire body, which Laurence said was a good thing, as it was drawing the illness out. However, I was due to go to a dance music festival in Portugal at the end of the month and knew I wouldn't be able to travel in that condition. So I told Laurence that I would be reverting to the steroid cream. When I did, my skin quickly returned to normal, and I was able to enjoy the festival.

I dig out Laurence's number and call him up, then make the

two-hour journey down to his North London practice a few days later. On checking my pulses and examining my tongue, the standard diagnostic techniques of Chinese Medicine, he tells me that my case is quite complicated, but he believes he can help.

In his early fifties, Laurence is divorced and has been working with Chinese Medicine for the last fifteen years. He's well-spoken with a Cambridge education and a vast knowledge of all things Shakespeare, about whom he's currently writing a second book. In a previous life, he'd found success running his own theatre company—a high-stress, super-demanding job, he tells me whilst inserting a needle into my wrist, sending fiery daggers up my arm.

After having a spiritual awakening through a near-death experience, Laurence decided that his work should reflect his new-found beliefs. He left the arts world and started training in acupuncture and Chinese herbs.

I decide early on to have two sessions a week. The cost of the treatment, plus the petrol, is going to be expensive, but I don't care. I just want to be healthy again, to have a life again, as soon as possible. The importance I used to place on having savings as security is irrelevant now. What's the point of having money if I can't enjoy it? Apparently, this is the occasion for which I'd been saving.

His treatment immediately starts to have an effect on me. I wouldn't have believed it possible. Yet after just one session, the pain and itching intensify. At night, the oozing that was previously confined to my face and neck now occurs all over my body, waking me up soaking wet with a substance that smells of death and decay.

Every single day on waking, I'm confronted with the same feeling: utter terror. My arms and legs, face and neck are so stiff it's as though my body has been set in concrete. I lie perfectly still for ten minutes, trying to summon the courage to move, trying not to think about the pain to come.

Finally, I throw off my duvet and hobble to the shower. Once under the water, my skin slowly starts to become supple. I gently rub off the layers of encrusted ooze. My body is so tender that no products can be used on it. Water alone must suffice.

Whilst under the spray, I can almost relax, except I know what is to come once I turn off the warm, soothing water. As I step from the shower, the fierce burning, itching flares up instantly. I can't rub my skin dry. I must dab at it, then dash back and lie on my bed, a million needles pricking my entire body. After another ten minutes of lying perfectly still, trying with all my might to focus on anything but the itching, I reach for my moisturising cream and apply it liberally from head to toe. Although the cream makes me exceptionally hot which heightens the torment, I wouldn't be able to eventually move without it. After lying on my bed for another twenty minutes, I carefully get to my feet to accomplish my next task.

I must fetch the vacuum cleaner and hoover up all the dead skin that's fallen off my body since the previous day. A thick film covers my sheets and floor. I'm always shocked by how much skin I lose every day.

Next, I must switch the sheets around so that I can use the same ones for at least a few days. The mattress, equally stained, I struggle to flip over. I focus solely on carrying out the task at hand, aware that the moment I stop I won't be able to get up again for some time. Which would suit me fine, as I'd just as well lie on my bed forever, never having to move another muscle again. While my body cracks and weeps, my mind swells with fear, anger and sadness. I hate my body, and I hate my life with a violence that frightens me.

With a tremendous force of will, I continue my daily rituals, gently sliding my body into trousers and a long-sleeved top. Shorts and a t-shirt would be less distressing. However, I'm doing all I can to hide the extent of the illness from my parents.

After dressing, I head downstairs for breakfast, hoping they aren't in the kitchen. I'm ashamed about how I look as if it's somehow my fault. Unfortunately, my mom is at the table, so I avoid facing her, holding a conversation with my head in the cupboard and then the fridge. I eat rapidly and head back upstairs where I sit as still as I can, watching hour after hour of mind-numbing daytime TV.

Some days, if I'm feeling extra brave, I head out into the woods a few miles away. Occasionally, the itching abates enough for me to appreciate the serene surroundings. More often than not, however, I find myself clenching my teeth against the pain as I strain to move with each step. When I can't take it any longer, I go home and join my parents for dinner. The heat of the food intensifies the itching and burning.

"How was Sutton Park?" my mom asks. "Were there many people about?"

"A few," I reply, shovelling food into my mouth.

"Which gate did you go in?"

"Four Oaks."

"I always go to Banners Gate. Anna likes to go on the swings. You'll have to come with us next time," she says, mentioning my six-year-old niece.

"Yeah, maybe," I reply, feeling guilty for the sullenness of my responses. In such pain, I can't taste the food I'm eating, let alone hold a conversation.

"We're going to go to Wales next week, to the caravan. You'll have to come and see it once you're feeling a bit better. The garden's looking lovely with all the new plants and there are loads of birds around at the moment," my mom says, persevering with the conversation.

"Okay," is all I can manage.

"I'm so sorry," I want to cry out. "Please forgive me for everything. I have caused you so much pain, so much heartache. I never meant to, I love you both so much."

Instead, all I can do is mumble, "thanks," and disappear back upstairs.

At night I continue to battle insomnia. My nervous system is racked with illness. I'm sure this is where the eczema stems from. My body twitches and jumps for hours on end. Dawn is breaking when sleep finally comes for me, and I'm able to forget about my life for a few blissful hours.

* * *

The only change to my daily routine comes on Tuesdays and Saturdays when I drive to London to see Laurence. These are the most difficult days. At the petrol station, the once-simple task of filling the tank requires untold strength. Every single movement tears into my raw flesh. But no petrol means no acupuncture and no chance of ever getting better.

I'm all too aware of my appearance—my face, hands and neck (the only areas of my skin visible) glowing like the embers of a fire. I know I must look ghastly, but what anyone thinks is the least of my worries.

Once back in the car, I start driving immediately, suppressing as best I can the desire to scratch. I know from experience that the second I succumb to it I may not be able to stop for hours. I speed along the motorway at 80 mph. Today, I manage to hold out for twenty minutes until the itching becomes too overwhelming. I attack my leg ferociously. All the way to London I cannot stop scratching despite the imminent danger.

"Whatever it takes," I shout. "I will never, ever give up." Only this complete conviction enables me to keep going.

By the time I get there, the floor of my car is filled with dead skin. After sitting still for a while and taking long, slow, deep breaths to calm body and mind, I open the car door. From then on, I try as hard as possible not to think, just move.

One more step, Mark. Keep going, one more step. Almost there. I repeat this mantra over and over so that I cannot feel the hot pokers searing my body and the knives slashing into my joints. I arrive at the clinic, relieved to see Laurence's affable smile. Simply being in his calm, reassuring presence helps me feel a little better. The acupuncture treatment certainly isn't pleasant but it doesn't matter given what I'm accustomed to living with.

"Every night this foul stuff oozes from my body," I tell him.

"Excellent," he replies. "It sounds like the illness is starting to come out. Be patient. Over time, the colour should become lighter and the oozing should eventually stop altogether."

He tells me of an ancient Chinese saying regarding the treatment of illness through acupuncture:

"Better: good," he says in an exaggerated, comedic Chinese accent. "Worse: good. Same: bad."

My cheeks burn as I smile for the first time in a long while.

"Change is positive, even if it seems to be worse initially," Laurence explains. One of the few people with whom I'm able to share my jungle experiences, he's fascinated by my tales of ayahuasca.

"There seems to be a link between that and the work you do," I tell him. "Both are ancient systems based on healing at an energetic level."

"That's right. The Chinese believe that all bodies have a life force energy called Qi, and all illness is the result of the impairment in the flow of this Qi. The needles work by manipulating and balancing this energy."

"Sounds fairly similar to what Hamilton was talking about when he discussed the straightening of crossed energies," I reply.

"I believe so. The acupuncture works on the mind, body and spirit simultaneously. That's how mental, physical and emotional problems can be addressed. Just like with ayahuasca, in this practice we don't make a distinction between the emotional and physical."

A few more weeks pass, and my condition continues to deteriorate. Although I believe in Laurence, I'm right at my limit. As I lie in bed surrounded by blood, fluid and dead skin, my mind conjures images of the machetes that are commonplace in the jungle. I fantasise about hacking off my limbs.

One morning, I come out of the bathroom after taking a shower and collapse on the floor, clawing at my legs in a frenzy. An hour goes by before I return to my feet. I continue scratching late into the evening. *I don't want to die*, I think, *but I cannot go on living like this much longer.*

Even though I've begun to believe in God, it gives me no comfort. I cry out in desperation, "Help me, please God. Help me. Where are you? I need you now." But even He is not listening.

I rack my brain for an answer. I remember hearing about how hypnosis can help with pain relief and wonder if it can do the same for itching. I find a local practitioner online and make an appointment immediately.

The hypnotist tells me that not only can he help with the itching, but he can also cure the eczema. He relates his previous successes, including the complete curing of a patient's skin condition in only six weeks.

In the first session, I slip into what he describes as a light trance.

For me, it's a profound state of relaxation during which the itching ceases. That same evening, I have a vivid dream, like none I've dreamed before. I'm standing before a mystical-looking man dressed in white robes. He has a large egg in his hands. In a blinding flash, he transforms it into a stunning, huge white horse. I mount the beast. We ride under a large expanse of water, then surface, riding above the ocean and off into the most breath-taking sunset I've ever seen. I'm bathed in bliss. I awake euphoric.

I consult Laurence for an interpretation. Glowing with comfort and peace he tells me, "This is the beginning of the journey of your spirit, an awakening of consciousness that will culminate in the blissfulness of the dream."

I cannot even imagine how that could come about.

"Ultimately, it is love that heals," he concludes, patting me on the shoulder.

I have no idea what he means.

* * *

Thoughts of Peru never totally leave my mind. As the months pass, the appeal grows, nudging me away from the disparaging vision of myself, pitted against a hateful world, toward a serene, compassionate person, surrounded by love. Only with Laurence's support can I maintain the faith that there's more to life than suffering.

I spend hours staring out of my window. I'm fascinated by my neighbour's tree, its trunk arching toward the sky with branches outstretched, welcoming the sun. As winter turns to spring, bare branches give way to budding leaf growth. The warmth of midsummer brings flowers bursting into full bloom. The walls of my prison cell are closing in on me, the air stale and stagnant. My parents' garden is a riot of colour. Rather than take in the beauty of the burgeoning outside world, I take it as a personal affront.

The leaves outside turn yellow, wither and fall to the ground, as another year of my life comes to an end. Over the last couple of months, the acupuncture has helped my condition improve enough to enable me to mark my birthday by going for a meal and a pint of lager with friends who I've not seen all year. I'm able to sit in the pub for a couple of hours before the discomfort gets the better of me, and I must return to my bed. With the passing of another year, it strikes me that it may take many years for me to get better, if I'm lucky.

I think again of ayahuasca. Also a form of energy healing, its intensity suggests to me that it could work faster than acupuncture. For now, the thought of having to go through that literally gut-wrenching experience again is enough to make me stick with the current treatment in the hope that a miracle will happen.

Instead, my condition deteriorates once more—the oozing, which had stopped after a couple of months, returns with a vengeance, preventing me from sleep for four days straight. On the drive down to London to see Laurence, my eyes drift shut several times. A crash seems inevitable. I'm too tired to care.

Somehow I arrive unscathed. When I enter Laurence's consultation room, I can barely hold back the tears.

"I just can't go on like this anymore," I tell him. "I've reached my limit. I'm going to stop the treatment and go back to the jungle."

As caring as ever, Laurence replies softly, "I understand. I won't charge you for this treatment." His voice falters just enough to make me wonder if he too is on the verge of tears, "Best of luck with everything. Please keep in touch."

As with my parents, I feel sorry for him and guilty, as though I've let him down.

* * *

To withstand the journey back to Peru, I resort once again to steroid cream. This time, it makes little difference. This time, I make an appointment at a local private hospital to see someone as quickly as possible. To prove the extent of my illness and ensure that I'm given something that actually works, I stop using the steroid cream for the three days prior to the appointment.

Once again, every inch of my skin burns like I've been dowsed in boiling oil. The slightest movement sears me through to the core and my skin feels like it's ripping apart. The night before the appointment, I hang on hour after hour, telling myself, "Tomorrow this will all be over," as the putrid liquid flows freely from my infected left arm.

When morning finally arrives I must pry myself from the sheets. I may be in a similarly desperate state, but the specialist is completely different. Dr. Basu is gentle, benevolent and most importantly, actually listens to me. I actually believe him when he says he can help me.

Two days later, the steroid pills he prescribed enable me to move without excruciating pain. He suggests I spend a week in the hospital to monitor my condition. Even though a dismal hospital is the last place I want to be, it's the only way I can get the treatment and medication necessary to return to Peru.

The stark, white room contains five other beds, all of which are occupied. Each has a curtain for privacy and a TV, which can be rented by the day for an exorbitant fee. The nurse offers me some filthy, oversized pyjamas that I politely decline, thankfully having brought my own.

"Welcome," says the man across the way, "I'm John." He's around fifty and of Indian descent. I think it unlikely that "John" is his given name.

"Hi," I reply shyly without meeting his eyes. "I'm Mark."

The others also introduce themselves. I'm by far the youngest patient here. I quickly learn the medical history of my fellow roommates. They've all suffered from terrible skin diseases for their whole lives.

"I've been in and out of this place for the last twenty-five years," John tells me. "These days I spend about half of my life in here. They've tried every treatment and they still can't get rid of my eczema." He sounds almost proud of its severity.

There is a genuine feeling of warmth and solidarity amongst the patients, though I don't want to join their club. As inspiring as their bravery and acceptance of their condition is, living with this disease is not an option for me.

Every morning, a new doctor appears to take my history. Twice a day, a nurse comes round to administer treatments—smothering me in the same steroid cream I've been using all along, the only difference being the massive quantity. Fortunately, this large amount offers me a little relief. It doesn't matter how temporary it may be, as long as I'm well enough to travel. It's so obvious to me that these endless rounds of appointments and applications of creams are a dulling suppression, a dead end. My mind and body scream it's time to get out of this world now—time to go and discover true healing.

At the end of the week, a doctor assesses everyone to see whether they're well enough to go home or whether they have to be moved to a ward in the main hospital. I'm deemed well enough to leave. Many of my companions are not so lucky. For John, it's his seventh straight week in hospital and there's no likelihood of him going home anytime soon.

I'm sent on my way with instructions to keep using the steroid cream until my follow-up appointment with Dr. Basu. With the frequent use of liberal quantities, it's possible to keep the eczema under the surface enough to get around. However, the internal furnace never ceases to roar, and every move continues to prick my skin with itchy needles.

As soon as I return home, I go online to see when the next Blue Morpho tour starts. There's one in a week. I wait a couple of days to see if my skin gets any worse. When it doesn't, I sign up and book a flight.

I suspect that it may take a few weeks, or maybe even months, of ayahuasca before I'm healed. I tell my parents that I'm going to try a plant-based medicine that has the ability to remove the root cause of my eczema by working at the body's energetic level—something that Western medicine simply cannot do. I don't want to lie to them, so I give them a small part of the truth. The rest will have to wait for another day. That way even if they don't believe what I'm saying, at least they won't be able to argue with the results. If I start talking to them about spirits and witchcraft, they'll think I've gone insane. And the last thing I want is for them to be subjected to the same terror that I've been feeling for over a year.

All my hopes for recovery lie with Hamilton and ayahuasca. I've left my parents house in England only a handful of times over the last twelve months. And now, I'm flying halfway round the world to the Amazon jungle. I manage a small smile at the sheer madness of it.

CHAPTER 5
The First Thirty Years

My childhood memories are not especially vivid. I'm told I was a very sickly baby, born prematurely with jaundice, then developing severe eczema at three months of age. The eczema lasted for three years, but I have no recollection of it. Nor do I remember that for the first five years of my life, I refused to leave my mom's side and would cry if we were separated for even a couple of minutes.

I experienced no great traumas as a child. The worst thing that happened was being burgled twice within a year, which prompted us to move house. The second time, my mom was inconsolable and adamant about leaving, as we'd all been asleep upstairs during the burglary. But all I remember is the policemen with their strange brushes and powder, checking the house for fingerprints.

Growing up I was happiest with a cricket bat in my hand or a football at my feet. I was a well-behaved child, too scared of being punished to ever get up to any mischief. Primary school came and went with few problems—I was always one of the top students, especially when it came to Maths. I loved numbers and statistics, hated anything to do with art or creativity.

I considered the mysteries of life from an early age. When I was eight, I looked up at the clouds passing by and wondered, *What's on the other side of the sky?* I decided it must be a brick wall. That answer satisfied me for an afternoon until I had another thought, *What's on the other side of the brick wall?*

"That stupid question led you to ayahuasca," Hamilton told me twenty years later.

When I was eleven, we were given a note for our parents to sign, requesting consent to allow their child to watch a series of videos about sex education. My parents never discussed sex with me. And I never asked them about it. As a result I didn't know anything other than it was something intensely embarrassing. So I waited until my parents were both outside before leaving the note on the kitchen table and dashing upstairs. In the morning, the signed note was right there waiting for me in the same place I'd left it. Nothing was ever said about it. This is the earliest recollection I have of the fear of sexual intimacy that was to shape my adult life.

That same year, I passed the Eleven Plus exam and gained a place at an all-boys school with a reputation for academic success. It was an old school trying hard to hang on to an outdated tradition in a modern world. Football was outlawed, rugby instead being the sport of choice. The teachers wore gowns and always had to be address as 'Sir'. Whenever they entered the room, pupils were expected to stand. Many of the teachers reflected the school's austere image, believing that intimidation and bullying were the most effective teaching methods. For some kids, this may've been the case. For a sensitive child like me, it was not.

My first-year English teacher, Mr. Walker, was a prime example of the school's philosophy. Known as "Piggy" for his striking resemblance to the animal, he would walk up and down the desks as we worked, flicking my ears or knocking my elbow off the desk. He relished creating an atmosphere of tension and fear. He would always mock my high-pitched voice and small stature.

Thankfully, in summer there was cricket, and being a decent opening batsman and occasional bowler, I always made the team. I treasure the memory of the smell of freshly cut grass on a hot summer's afternoon, as I waited with an equal amount of anxiety and excitement for the game to start. Years later in the Amazon, whenever we drove along the Iquitos - Nauta highway to camp and passed recently trimmed grass, I would instantly be transported back to a cricket pitch in Walsall.

As the years passed, interest and conversation turned from

sport to girls. Unfortunately, at an all-boys school there wasn't much opportunity to meet them. Whenever my sister, who was two years older than I, brought a friend home I would turn mute. On one occasion, my dad refused to take me to football training unless I said, "Hello" to her friend Maria. It took me a couple of hours to find the courage to say that one word. By the time I managed to blurt it out, I was shaking. Solely the fear of missing my beloved football practice enabled me to say it at all.

Our family summer holidays in the south of France were the only times I got to meet girls. Just before my fifteenth birthday I had my first kiss in the darkness of her parents' caravan. Our lips met, and for one glorious moment time stopped. Having no idea what to do next, I opened my mouth and our teeth clashed together for what felt like an eternity before I pulled away. I wanted nothing more than to run away from her and never look back. Yet I stood there paralysed, eyes fixed on my shoes, and mumbled, "Thanks."

Not long after, I had my first date with a girl named Sue. A week after being introduced by a mutual friend, she phoned me up and asked me out to the cinema. When the fateful day arrived, I realised I had no clue how to talk to girls. As we sat watching Kylie Minogue in The Delinquents, I spent the first half of the film trying to pluck up the courage to put my arm around her, only to abandon the effort as too difficult. We sat in silence watching the movie, tension building between us with each passing minute. As soon it ended, she left without so much as a goodbye. I followed at a distance in case she was going to wait for me outside. But she just kept walking, crushing any semblance of self-confidence I had.

While my friends started having girlfriends, I remained unable to cope with the demands of adolescence. Yet, I kept up the appearance of a "normal" person on the outside. No one realised what a mess

I was on the inside. I became so skilled at hiding it that I too became detached from my feelings and the extent of my problems.

I'd come to believe that it was absolutely impossible for me to change, to become a real man. I wanted nothing more than to disappear from this life in which I had no right to be happy or have good things happen to me. Essentially, I didn't believe I deserved to exist. Back then I never would've imagined that so many years later, in the depths of Peruvian Amazon, my life would literally depend on addressing these very same issues.

* * *

Before I could reach that point, I went through years of drinking and doing drugs, starting at Nottingham University, which was as famous for its social life as for its academic success. Having been placed in a men's hall of residence, I concentrated more on the social scene since parties were the best place to meet girls. I was no longer so timid because I had discovered a secret weapon to overcome my shyness—beer!

Alcohol was my answer for everything that worried me, especially dealing with the scariest situation of all—being in the company of women. However, by the time I was drunk enough to chat a girl up, I was usually too wasted to hold a coherent conversation. Or stand up, for that matter. There were the occasional evenings when I got "lucky". By morning, when the alcohol wore off the paralysing fear returned. The one thing I truly wanted in life petrified me more than anything else: to love and be loved. Without alcohol, I would've been even lonelier and more despondent. It never crossed my mind that I had a problem; this was university and everyone drank, often excessively. It was expected. I was just having fun.

After gaining my degree, I put off going into the real world and stayed on for another year to do a Masters in Environmental Management. Studying was one thing, having the discipline to get up and go to work every day was quite another.

Environmental Management had a large component of self-study, which left plenty of spare time to spend at The Wheatsheaf. Not your average student hangout, The Wheatsheaf was a dirty, run down "locals" pub with a free pool table.

An eclectic mix of the unemployed, ex-criminals, alcoholics, invalided war veterans, over-the-top gay drama queens and men who didn't want to go home to their wives, The Wheatsheaf was a pub you wouldn't return to if you happened to walk in off the street. It soon became my second home. My mates and I became friends with many of the regulars, most of whom spent even longer there than we did. There was a familial atmosphere, albeit a dysfunctional one, which was a rare find.

The social event of the year was The Wheatsheaf Christmas party. In attendance was my girlfriend Emily, a third-year psychology student whom I'd known vaguely for the last couple of years. Recently, we'd become closer, sharing as we did an interest in drinking beer, playing pool and generally hanging out at The Wheatsheaf. It was common practice for us to end the evening either at my house or hers, drunkenly feasting on the king of student foods, oven chips.

A tall, straight-talking, out-going girl with a dry wit, Emily was someone I fancied quite a lot and assumed the feeling was mutual. Unfortunately, I was too shy to find out for sure. On several occasions, we even shared a bed. Rather than seizing the opportunity, I fetched a sleeping bag for myself. One evening as we lay together on her sofa, she asked through pursed lips, "What do you want to happen between us?"

Immediately sent into panic mode, I looked into space and muttered, "I dunno."

"Do you want to just be friends?" she pressed, looking me straight in the eye.

"Erm, I don't think so," I managed to reply.

And with that, she did what I should've had the courage to do weeks before—she kissed me.

I was shocked. I couldn't believe anyone would really want to go out with me, that anyone could like me that much, even with all the evidence to the contrary. It didn't matter what Emily said or did, nor how much she tried to coax me into opening up. I couldn't do it. Instead, I dealt with my intimacy issues by drinking more, until I was doing it every day.

I was terrified of sex. I was not only certain I wouldn't be any good but also far too embarrassed to talk to Emily, or anyone, about it. I figured if I drank enough alcohol I would lose my inhibitions enough to do it. However, I lost more than my inhibitions. Some mornings I couldn't even remember whether or not we'd had sex. Ironically, Emily was such a caring, considerate person that, had I been able to communicate with her, I may have been able to resolve my issues.

"You can only love other people to the extent that you love yourself," Hamilton told me years later.

My relationship with Emily continued on and off until the following September. The fact that she held out so long is a testament to her kindness and patience. When she told me that she didn't want to see me anymore, I didn't utter a single word. I felt no anger, no sadness. Nothing. I stood frozen in place, staring at the wall, unable to meet her gaze or even move until she left half an hour later.

* * *

After completing my Masters degree, I started work in Nottingham as a trainee computer programmer, thus rendering my four years of study completely irrelevant. Life continued much as before, though the drinking was now reserved for weekends, mostly. I met another amazing girl, only for our relationship to come to a similarly dismal end.

One day, as I sat at my desk at work, staring vacantly around the office, I asked Sam, my friend and colleague, "Don't you think there's more to life than this?" Pointing out some of our older colleagues, I continued, "Look at these guys. That'll be us in twenty or thirty years."

"I quite like working here to be honest," he replied. "It pays well and it's an easy, low-stress job. There's a lot worse places to work."

"True. But come on, the thought of sitting here, typing code into this computer until I retire scares the crap out of me. Being financially secure with a nice house and car isn't enough for me."

Sam looked like he had no idea what I was talking about so I shut up. With little desire for promotion and no chance of getting laid off, there was no incentive to overextend myself. The last thing I wanted to do was fall into a routine and before I knew it, become an old man, still working there, still single, doing nothing with my life.

At that time, everything was about making it to the weekend—those two days of freedom when I could forget about the supposed real world and go out drinking. Now that I was no longer a student and had to fit most of my alcohol consumption into two evenings, I made the most of them. By the end of every Friday and Saturday night, I would be blind drunk and frequently unable to remember large portions of the night. It became commonplace for me to wake up with an all-too-familiar feeling of dread, knowing that I'd said or done something I shouldn't, without having any idea what it was. Countless times I heard: "Do you remember what you did last night?" accompanied by a knowing smirk that always made me break out in a cold sweat.

After several years, I decided to leave my current life and unhealthy ways behind. I went travelling for a year, to Australia and New Zealand. I chose these destinations because they speak the same language, more or less. Regardless, travelling was a daunting prospect. At the same time, I knew that doing it was vital to my physical and mental well-being.

Nobody will know who I am. I will be free to be someone totally new, the person I've always wanted to be.

And so, in March 2000 I headed for Melbourne, ready for big, positive changes. In the hostels there were always so many young, carefree people, along with cheap bottles of wine and parties to attend. After a few months of that lifestyle, I sought healthier pursuits, preferring instead to cycle through the wilderness of Tasmania and hike in the New Zealand countryside.

In addition to having a great time while I was there, my confidence grew, and my ideas about what I was capable of started to shift. At the end of the trip I did grow into a healthier person, somewhat. But I also discovered that transforming myself into someone new isn't as simple as leaving the country. I thought I'd return home happy, ready to get on with my life. Instead, those twelve months abroad were only the beginning of a much longer journey that would culminate many years later in a wooden hut in the Peruvian Amazon.

On returning home, I got another computer programming job, this time in London. The pay and benefits were excellent. The work was interesting and not stressful. My co-workers were all lovely. If I wanted, there were plenty of opportunities for progression. The company was committed to looking after its staff and ran a multitude of courses designed to help us develop both technical and personal skills. My boss, no doubt aware of my great need for them, encouraged me to go on a variety of *soft skills* courses: assertiveness training, communication skills, self-development etc. Just the words "soft skills" made me cringe and want to run and hide because I would have to put myself on show and no doubt be judged.

Since I hadn't lived the healthiest of lifestyles whilst travelling, I took up jogging to get back into shape. Two weeks later, being a man of moderation and reasonable expectations, I decided to run the London Marathon. And merely completing the marathon wouldn't be enough either. I had to do it in the quickest time possible. Whether it be partying, studying or exercising, there was only one way to go: hard.

From the very beginning, I was dedicated to the regime, clocking up thirty to thirty-five miles a week in four sessions. For eight months training was my life. Everything else had to fit in around it, even the socialising and drinking. I loved the buzz of feeling fit and having lots of energy.

Running down The Mall for the final few hundred yards I saw my mom, sister and niece waving from the grandstand. As I crossed the finish line, I was relieved and reasonably happy, but not ecstatic, like many of the other runners. I completed the race in three hours, forty minutes with plenty of energy to spare. Rather than be proud of my time and endurance, all I could think about was that I should've run it faster.

Shortly thereafter, I abandoned running to experiment with yoga and Tai Chi. Then, I found my way to a beginner's meditation course at a Buddhist centre in West London. While I found the practice extremely frustrating, never managing to keep my concentration for more than a couple of seconds, I began going regularly. I found that when meditating with a group I was less distracted and felt brief moments of peace unlike anything I'd ever experienced before.

While I had a seemingly healthy lifestyle, I remained restless and troubled, unable to settle into my life in London. The more uncomfortable I felt, the more I wanted to travel. This time Latin America was calling.

I set to work learning Spanish and quickly fell in love with the language. In February 2004, I got on a plane to Mexico City.

CHAPTER 6
Ayahuasca – Ultimate Hope

"Will the ayahuasca be able to heal me?" I ask Hamilton, as we sit in his flat in the centre of Iquitos.

He takes a deep breath and fixes his gaze on me. "I have no idea," he replies. "I think it can help, but I can't give you any guarantees. It will at least help you come to terms with the illness."

"What's wrong with me? Can you see the cause?" I continue, knowing he has the ability to shift his consciousness and see people's energetic make-up.

"I can see that you have some crazy energy in you, but I don't know what it is. I think you're a very interesting case. You say you hate drinking ayahuasca, yet here you are again!

I'll give you this promise, though," he adds. "You're welcome to stay here, and I'll continue to help you for as long as you want, even if that's fifty years."

I'm delighted to discover that operations have recently moved to a new camp, only sixty kilometres by road from Iquitos. It's a massive relief to have only a one-and-a-half-hour bus ride instead of the previous eighteen-hour river journey.

Our transport is an antiquated, comical-looking wooden bus, open at the sides and adorned with gaudy figures of Jesus and the Virgin Mary. Once inside, we take our places on the hard seats, glad to have plenty of room to spread out. Even though I'm pretty small, I occupy the majority of a seat designed for two people. Peruvians certainly don't have the same issues with personal space as we in the West.

The bus turns off the highway and bumps along the rough, narrow track that leads to our home for the next eight days. In the early stages of building, this new camp is large and luxurious by jungle standards. The main house, designed for eating and holding ceremonies, is almost twice the size of the old one. The bathroom facilities, sleeping quarters and a kitchen are off to the back of the main room. There are also three other bungalows, large enough for a total of a dozen people.

Built to withstand years of downpours, all are made of local timber with leaf roofs painstakingly handwoven together. The tightly sewn mesh ensures no mosquitoes or other bugs will disturb us here. That alone is enough to make me fall in love with the place.

Hamilton has big plans for expansion. Eventually, the camp will comfortably accommodate twenty-four guests. In the last couple of months, business has begun to pick up. Ten guests will be participating in ceremony this week, along with Hamilton, Don Alberto and their four apprentices.

"The spirits told me a long time ago that an article would one day be published about us in National Geographic and when that happened, demand would increase dramatically," Hamilton tells me.

On the table lies the current edition of National Geographic Adventure magazine. A former guest who overcame a lifetime of acute depression and suicidal ideation in just five ceremonies wrote an extensive article about Hamilton and Blue Morpho. Although she came solely for her own healing, the profoundness of her experience inspired her to share the story with the world.

* * *

As the first ceremony approaches, I do my best to cultivate a positive state of mind and push away my doubts and concerns.

Do you want to live with this eczema for the rest of your life?

A brief visualisation of what this would be like is all the motivation I need to stay focused during the night ahead. Before I enter the main house, I take a deep cleansing breath, feeling my shoulders drop.

SHEDDING THE LAYERS

I choose the mattress closest to the toilets—even a few extra yards can make a big difference once in the grip of the medicine.

"Buenas noches, buenas noches," says Alberto with a little hand wave, as he enters clutching his plastic bag containing cigarettes and mapachos.

Shortly after drinking the ayahuasca, the customary feelings of disorientation surface and fear starts to penetrate my entire body. *It's okay. I've done this before. Nothing bad is going to happen. It's just the medicine working.* I try to let the cascade of emotions wash over me without resisting. However, the force of the ayahuasca pounds me relentlessly, and sweat begins to soak through my clothes and drip from my forehead. I lose all sense of my identity. I career headlong towards oblivion. In my last moment of awareness, I cry out to Hamilton for help.

Then, the room is gone and there is only chaos. A thousand thoughts and images flash through my mind, far too quickly to make any sense of them. My ability to think has been obliterated. I'm lost in a spinning world of insanity. I shout and have no idea what I'm saying. A terrific force within threatens to rip my chest clean open.

And then water is falling on me and I'm shivering. Cold tiles beneath me tell me that I'm in a shower. I rise unsteadily to my feet and shut the water off.

"How are you doing now?" A familiar voice asks from outside.

"I'm okay. I think," I reply, trying to work out who's out there as a towel is passed around the curtain. I dry myself off and look out to see Chris's amiable face and bald head. I remember where I am. Chris is one of Hamilton's part-time apprentices.

"That was pretty wild for a time," he says. "Do you remember anything about it?"

"I remember going totally crazy," I tell him. "And I have the vague recollection of somebody being near me, talking to me, but that's about it."

"That was me. I came over to help you. That dark spirit hit you pretty hard. You threw off all your clothes—well, other than the t-shirt you're still wearing—and you were thrashing around violently. You almost ended up on top of the girl next to you."

News to me.

"I started singing icaros and you kept trying to grab the shacapa out of my hand. Your face became contorted, and you looked possessed," he informs me.

"Sorry about that," I say sheepishly.

"That's okay," he replies, "All part of the job. If you're okay, I'm going to go to bed now. The ceremony finished some time ago. You should get some rest too."

The next day, Don Alberto tells me that a tremendous demon inside me caused the fierce reaction. He says that it came from the witchcraft and has now left me, never to return. I'm relieved and thrilled to hear this, reasoning that this must have been the cause of my eczema. Now I must be healed.

Yet again, I'm to be disappointed. Alberto says that although this demon has now gone, the witchcraft has left behind what he terms *mal* (Spanish for "bad"). Which he describes as a kind of spiritual phlegm that has spread throughout my entire body, causing the physical illness. He reckons it may take six months to remove it all.

Six months!? I can't stay here that long, I think, knowing that I have no choice in the matter. Just one more ayahuasca ceremony seems too many, let alone dozens of them.

I swing restlessly in the hammock as the afternoon hours pass. The closer it gets to dusk, the stronger my desire to flee screaming down the highway grows. I do a succession of Sudoku puzzles in an attempt to distract myself from the horrific memories of past ceremonies.

As the week progresses, I spend each night fighting to remove the illness. My body constantly feels like glue is running throughout it. My bones ache and my nervous system leaves me twitchy and restless. Plus, the barrage of negativity continues to assault me: *I can't be healed. It's too hard. I don't deserve to be healthy.* Thousands of thoughts a minute whizz by like cars on a motorway as I stand dazed in the midst of them.

During this particular ceremony, however, after hours of this mental bombardment, something shifts. I realise that these thoughts are not actually me, rather a multitude of dark spirits that I've collected on life's journey. The reality that they've created for me— a distortion of the truth—led to years of unhappiness and longing. Now I see that the decision to believe these, or any thoughts, is a choice. And the choices I make directly create my life experience.

* * *

During this first week, I manage to participate in all five ceremonies. Each time I drink, my physical condition deteriorates. By the end of the week, my skin is red and blotchy, cracked and oozing, and both of my ears hurt and are infected. Half of the palm of my left hand is filled with pus. My scalp, like my legs, is raw and bleeding and also probably has an infection. The ayahuasca wants the illness out, while the steroid cream is trying to keep it in. The cream is no match for the ayahuasca.

Alberto says that he doesn't want me taking any antibiotic tablets, as these will clash with the ayahuasca. At least I'm able to use antibiotic drops in my ears and ointment on my skin. Clearly, continuing with the steroid cream is pointless. As scared as I am about not using it again, I know I have to let the illness out to get better.

To continue my healing, the maestro instructs me to complete a shamanic diet on the next workshop. Whilst on the diet, only a certain type of river fish, boquichico, and plantain are eaten (no salt, oil or other condiments are allowed), along with *fariña*, a drink made from fermented yuca, a starchy root vegetable found in the jungle.

While the food may be unappetising and the thought of tree spirits living inside my body forever is disconcerting, my main objection is that we're not allowed to use any products on our bodies for the duration of the diet. Which means no moisturising cream. While I know it is possible to survive without steroid cream, going without the moisturiser is impossible—within a few hours my skin would be so cracked and sore that I wouldn't be able to move any part of my body. Mimi and Daniel, another full-time apprentice, tell me that when the time comes, they will do everything they can to help, including carry me around if necessary.

My condition continues to worsen each day during the six-day break I spend in Iquitos. *All I have to do is make it through eight more days at camp.* No matter how many times I tell myself this, I still don't believe it.

* * *

A typical shamanic diet consists of a number of different plants, but I am to diet only sanango. This plant is known for its efficacy for treating physical ailments. Unlike other diets that use tree barks, twelve roots of the sanango plant are distilled and drunk. As each tree has only one root, a dozen will die for my participation in this process.

SHEDDING THE LAYERS

Since sanango is traditionally drunk during the night, I rise at 2 a.m. and place a mattress and a plastic bowl on the floor of my bungalow. I then apply as much moisturiser as my skin will take and wait for the shaman. Don Alberto greets me with a chuckle, mapacho in hand.

The tree roots have been infusing for several hours. Don Alberto pours me a dose of the yellow liquid, sings an icaro into it and covers it in smoke before silently handing it to me. I stare into the glass for a second, asking the spirits to heal me, then down it in three gulps.

I was warned that sanango was a hot and spicy plant, but nothing could have prepared me for this first taste. My stomach convulses as soon as the liquid hits. Instantly, I'm bathed in sweat and begin to salivate like a rabid dog. I long for just one sip of cool water, but this is forbidden. For the next hour, time and again I stumble dizzily to the toilet and back. Alberto stays with me, singing icaros until I collapse into a deep sleep, full of vivid dreams.

Stiff from head to toe, I hobble to the main house for breakfast. This is my first diet meal. The fish is mealy and filled with splintery bones. The plantain is dry and tasteless. The fariña smells like vomit. The food rises back up into my mouth as I consider having to eat it for the next eight days.

Tolerating the food is nothing compared to the condition of my skin. I seek out Hamilton to see if there may be some natural products that I can use to stay moisturised. I cannot last one day like this, let alone eight. He discusses the situation with Abuelo Sanango, the grandfather medicine spirit of the sanango plant, then tells me the spirit will allow me to use the moisturising cream. I feel the vice-like grip of tension in my body soften a little.

Alberto tells me that the sanango will cause my skin to peel. In snake-like fashion, I shed my entire body, from scalp to toes.

Whereas the snake emerges reborn with a bright new layer, my skin continues to peel, again and again, becoming more tender and raw. It's as though my entire self is being stripped away, leaving nothing but an exposed, hateful core.

My fingers are curled into permanent fists. Soles bare of all skin, I can only move on tiptoe. Days pass. Taking it one day at a time is way too daunting. One minute at a time is my limit, every second, an act of survival. My only thoughts: *trust the medicine, trust the diet.*

Tuesday morning finally arrives. Alberto gives me a spoonful of salt to swill round my mouth, thus marking the end of the diet. My body continues to deteriorate. As I lift my arms to change into a t-shirt, the skin around my armpits splits in several places. Tears stinging my eyes, I stumble outside and slip flat on my back in the mud, furious at what my life has become.

In his ever-calm demeanour, Alberto insists that the diet is working, that he can see the illness leaving.

"*La medicina te va a curar,*" he says deliberately. "The medicine will heal you."

* * *

Back in town, I go directly to the pharmacist to buy a supply of paracetamol and ibuprofen, as well as antihistamines for the itching. I take the maximum dose, curl into a ball on my bed and ask to be taken away from here.

I'm nine years old and have just been selected for my primary school football team, one of three boys in my year to make the grade. I puff out my chest as I run proudly into the playground in full kit: bright yellow jersey, blue shorts and yellow socks. The other kids look on jealously. I revel in the attention. Secretly, I imagine that there are 40,000 adoring fans, and I'm running onto the pitch at Villa Park, ready for my home debut for Aston Villa, the greatest team on the entire planet. The warmth of the afternoon sun beats down on my soft, flawless skin, transporting me to a place of pure happiness.

Daylight slices through the curtains, cutting short my dream. The memories linger for an instant, enabling me to relish the long-forgotten feelings of health, happiness and freedom. Just as quickly, relief gives way to reality. Panic surges through my body as I'm confronted with another day. I look at the sheets, white when I went to bed, now a translucent brown paste.

I strip the linen from the bed and screw it up into a ball, hoping that somehow this will make it look less disgusting to the cleaning lady. No matter, the mattress is just as drenched. The stench is sickening and the floor a patchwork of dead skin. I gulp down the painkillers to withstand the torment of the shower.

Two hours later the pain has lessened sufficiently to consider leaving the room. Once I've eaten and the room has been cleaned, I can relax in the knowledge that I won't have to move again for the rest of the day.

On my previous visit to Iquitos, I bought some trousers made by local indigenous women of the Shipibo tribe. At the time it seemed like an impulse buy, but now these paper-thin trousers are a real lifesaver since I can't expose my legs in shorts, and putting on regular trousers would be self-torture. Summoning all my courage, I venture outside of my air-conditioned refuge to go two entire blocks, to the restaurant.

On arrival I collapse into the chair, more thankful than when I finished the marathon. The stares of the other diners and waitresses bore into me from all directions as my body screams in distress. I focus on my breathing while I wait for the food to arrive.

After eating, I congratulate myself on another small victory. I direct my attention to the next task at hand. With the maid sure to still be hard at work, I shuffle across the square to the internet café.

Reading emails from friends at home lifts my spirits and helps maintain my determination to heal. I picture us all together at a country cottage that I've rented to celebrate my recuperation—we all sit around the dining table as I recount the story of my illness, the hardships I suffered, and how grateful I am for all the positive changes in my life. Not to mention that I survived. This image keeps alive the tiniest spark of hope that I can somehow recover.

Back at the hotel, the ever-friendly receptionist asks me how I'm doing.

How the fuck do you think I am? I want to yell. *Just give me the damn key.*

I reply, "*Bien*," my face twisted into a rictus grin, my body threatening to crumple to the ground.

As I reach my room and open the door, I undo my trousers with the other hand. In a flash they're on the floor, and I'm on the bed, scratching and scratching and scratching—the moment of a lifetime. As I persist, the skin cascades down, covering the bed and floor. But there's no stopping me. I'm like a drug addict getting his fix. The relief is absolute.

I don't move a muscle until morning when I must repeat my routine. Whilst showering, I notice hair all over the floor and on the bed sheets. Within a few days not a single hair remains on my arms, chest or legs.

Later in the week, it's obvious that the moisturising cream I brought isn't going to last much longer. I scour all the pharmacies in

Iquitos only to find that there's nothing remotely similar. I phone my mom and ask her to post me some. I pray that it arrives before I run out.

* * *

Next week at camp, Alberto prepares a different kind of treatment for me. Every afternoon I'm given a medicinal bath made from a number of different plants; this too is designed to draw out the illness. Heated on a fire, it's blessedly warm and soothing on what's left of my skin. I stand there while Mimi and Eluco, the third and final full-time apprentice, pour the concoction over my entire body.

Eluco is a short, well-built man with a wide, golden-toothed smile and a hearty laugh. Much younger looking than his forty years, Eluco served in the Peruvian army, training soldiers in jungle survival techniques. He also has a reputation for being a ladies' man. Whenever I ask him about it, he grins like a naughty schoolboy and tells me of his current stock of girlfriends.

The medicinal baths and meal times are the only occasions that I leave my bed. Each night as the others drink their ayahuasca I lie curled in a ball. I look down at my feet, now swollen to twice their normal size, and wonder when this madness will end.

My condition has worsened each day of the five weeks I've spent in Peru. I cannot even participate in the ceremonies that I came here for. If there were any other possible way of getting healthy I would take it now without question. All I want to do is quit. Yet it's not an option. Even if I wanted to go home, it is a physical impossibility.

I cry out, "It's too much. I can't do this anymore. Whatever I'm learning through this is not worth the pain. Take me back to my old, ignorant life. I may not have been happy, but it was better than this. Please, make the torture stop!"

* * *

I'm younger this time, maybe five or six, diving full-length across the carpet to make a fingertip save from my dad's fierce shot. I throw the ball back to him. This time the ball goes to my right. I pounce on it delightedly, and hold it aloft in triumph. My dad sits down on the sofa, beckoning me to come and join him. I dash across the living room and leap into his welcoming arms. I melt into his warm, strong body. Nothing can ever harm me, I am always protected.

In the morning I awake and wonder why my only memories of being happy are from my childhood. What went wrong later in life? There's no reason for me to feel this way.

My precious cream has dwindled to less than a day's supply. I don't have the energy to worry about what I'll do without it. I pray for death to come and take me. What comes for me instead is the package from my mom. Its arrival helps me find enough strength to get out of bed one more time.

CHAPTER 7
Into the Abyss

"There's only one way you're going to heal yourself," Hamilton tells me as we ride the bus out to camp. "You're going to have to start drinking ayahuasca again."

It's now mid-April, but with no real seasons in the jungle, time passes unnoticed. My existence has become suspended somewhere along the way. I'm trapped in a nether world between life and death. The air shimmers in the mid-morning heat, distorting the crumbling wooden shacks propped up on either side of the highway.

Hamilton's prediction has come true: business is booming. Group sizes have increased to twenty or more in the wake of the National Geographic article. In the centre of camp is a brand new building designed specifically to hold ceremonies. A rotund structure with a vaulted ceiling and thatched roof, it can hold over thirty people and soon will be running at capacity. In their leather, executive office chairs, flanked by the apprentices, the shamans look more like they should be preparing for a board meeting than an ayahuasca ceremony. The guests sit facing them in two semi-circles, one inside the other.

I'm finally well enough to take part in some of the ceremonies. I swallow my ayahuasca with the usual mixture of anticipation and fear. One thing is for certain: its taste hasn't improved in the ten weeks since I last drank it.

Oh my God, I think as the shamans start to build the energy in the room. I sense my state of consciousness changing. *How could I forget how terrifying and difficult this really is?* Fireworks are going off inside my head. All around I hear *Yes! Yes! Yes! Yes!* From within, my mind rebels, *No! No! No! No! Why the fuck am I doing this again?*

The three-dimensional patterns come quickly, engulfing me. Now, I'm flying through them, as if I'm inside a huge, multi-coloured machine. Completely at its mercy and terrified about where it's taking me, I wince and cringe as faces emerge from the patterns, racing towards me, one after another. They all have demonic features, some twisted in agony, some laughing menacingly. With each comes a corresponding emotion—sometimes anger, sometimes sadness, but most of the time raw fear. I cannot allow these evil forces to dominate me.

"Get out of my body, get out now. I'm not listening to you anymore. Leave. Leave. Now!" I yell inside my head.

But they're relentless. Seconds pass like hours as I fight for my life. They come at me in wave after wave, and I keep shouting. I have no idea what they are. All I know is they were inside me and now they're leaving. Fifteen months of struggle has created a deep reserve of fortitude. I need every drop of that now.

My attention pulled to my immediate surroundings, I become aware of a cacophony of sounds bouncing around the wooden hut. Shouting, screaming, crying and vomiting come from all directions as people confront their own demons. I'm inside an insane asylum.

And then I lose all sense of who I am, where I am and what I am doing. I cease to exist. There is nothing.

Finally, a faint noise way off in the distance begins to call me to return, gently bringing me back to conscious awareness. It is an icaro. Its melody penetrates my being. I offer no resistance to the hauntingly beautiful words:

Step into the light
Move away from the dark
Heal your mind
Live from the heart

Step into the light
Move away from the dark
Heal your mind
Live from the heart

I stand here now
My heart full of love
Pure medicine
Streaming down from above

I stand here strong
My teachers by my side
Divine light
Gives fear no place to hide

So send me more light
To keep me strong
So I can sing
This simple song

Step into the light
Move away from the dark
Heal your mind
Live from the heart

I manage a weak smile, feeling like a boxer slumped against the ropes. I'm exhausted and immensely thankful to still be in the ring.

"The warrior's only job is to survive the battle," Hamilton tells me.

* * *

SHEDDING THE LAYERS

A cool, refreshing breeze blows through the camp while I swing lazily in a hammock, the rhythm lulling me into a state of relaxation. The insects and birds call to each other as the afternoon passes gently by. I think about the last few ayahuasca experiences. Recently, there's been no screaming, thrashing or stripping naked—quite an improvement.

Tonight, as ever, I spend much of the ceremony on the toilet, much to the amusement of Alberto, who calls it "my office". As is quite typical when I'm here, I forget where I am, until I hear him shout "*¡Inglés!*" and start laughing. His nickname for me means "Englishman". *Right*, I think, *I'll get up in a minute*. Immediately I'm transported somewhere else in the ayahuasca realm and don't make it back to my seat until long after the ceremony has come to an end. The next day I estimate that I spent a full seven hours on my porcelain office chair.

"First I'm going to heal his skin. Then, I'm going to have to heal his hemorrhoids," Hamilton jokes with the guests.

Sitting on the toilet for so long is uncomfortable and has led me to seek out alternative positions. When fatigue sets in, I lower my head down between my knees as far as it will go, almost touching the floor and rest my arms behind me on the back of the toilet seat. I call this The Ski Jumper.

Another, more risky, posture is The Perch. Only employed after an especially long session, four hours or more, I move my backside toward the rear of the seat and rest my feet up on its front edge. This reduces discomfort in my legs but requires keen awareness and balance, as the danger exists of slipping down through the hole and becoming wedged. It's important to remember which bathroom I'm in, as some of the toilets have loose seats, which could precipitate a messy end to the evening.

I tell Hamilton about this search for comfort. He suggests that

I may have stumbled upon a new form of exercise: Toilet Yoga.

Through it all, the cycle of itching and scratching returns as strongly as ever. However deeply disturbing it is, I must accept that this is the healing process—a rollercoaster ride of recovery and relapse as the medicine brings the illness out from deep within my core.

* * *

Lying in my bed, I hear Hamilton's unmistakable voice carry from the main house across the otherwise silent camp. Forever in good spirits, he is laughing and joking with the other guests. I listen to him tell them about Blue Morpho.

"After my first ayahuasca ceremony, I knew I was in the place where I had to apprentice," he says. "I also knew that it was going to take a long time. So I needed a way to support myself. I made an agreement with the guide who took me out there: I would build a house for myself, and he could use it as a base for guests wanting to do jungle tours. Even though I didn't know anything about construction, the spirits taught me everything: how to build the house, how to put in the water system, and even how the septic tank would work. It was wild!

"The guide and I created Blue Morpho as a jungle adventure business, nothing to do with holding ayahuasca ceremonies for guests. I was the translator and jungle guide. In ceremonies I was just an apprentice. The shaman was the same guy I'd participated in my first ceremony with. Now and again a guest would come who was interested in ayahuasca, and the shaman allowed them to drink alongside me.

"We continued like this for a year, losing money every month. It became clear things weren't going to work out with my business partner. So we parted ways. And then, the shaman I'd been working with turned on me one night in ceremony and tried to kill me. Obviously, I survived but the next day became very sick and had to be evacuated from camp. I was totally convinced I was dying. On the ferry to Iquitos, I recorded a final message to my mom on my Dictaphone. Somehow, I made it back to the city and arrived at the hospital with a temperature of 108°F. The doctors diagnosed me with malaria and kept me in the hospital for observation. While I was there, I lost consciousness and had the classic near-death experience of travelling down the tunnel of white light. As I approached the point of no return I heard laughter and saw the shaman mocking me. I got so mad that I demanded to be sent back to my body—I wasn't going to let him kill me. So I came back and woke up. A few days later, the doctor discharged me, but I was still super sick. With no business and no master shaman, I had nowhere to go but home to the States.

"Most of the witchdoctors in the region where I apprenticed hated the fact that a white guy was learning the medicine. They all wanted me dead. I was the big prize. Soon, I realised that even in the States, I wasn't safe from attack. They would come after me spiritually as I sat in my mom's house in California. I knew the only way to make it stop was to return to the jungle and complete my apprenticeship. I had no intention of staying on afterwards to work as a master shaman. I just wanted to be able to defeat those witchdoctors so I could get on with my life back in America.

"When I got back to Peru, I found another shaman to work with. Unfortunately, our relationship fell apart as soon as I found out that she wanted me to marry one of her daughters and take care of her and her family. When I wouldn't do it, she turned on me too.

"Totally exhausted and defeated, I asked the spirits, 'What now?'

"They told me that Blue Morpho would become my healing

centre and that guests would come from all over the world to drink ayahuasca with me. I thought they were crazy. I was still sick from the witchdoctor attacks and had no master shaman. They told me to go and find Alberto who would teach me.

"I'd heard of Alberto before—he had a reputation for being a great healer—and so I went to his village of Jenaro Herrera and asked him if he would accept me as an apprentice. He didn't answer that day. But came back the next to tell me he'd spoken with his spirit guides, and if I could survive the training, he would teach me. Later, Alberto told me he'd had visions of a white guy coming to the jungle to learn the medicine ten years earlier, and he'd been waiting patiently for him to show up!"

There is a pause in the narrative as Hamilton lights his mapacho. He smokes in silence for a few seconds, the audience too captivated to say a word.

"If things hadn't been intense enough before, they soon got a whole lot crazier. Almost every ceremony, I'd be in a heinous witchdoctor battle with three or four of them at the same time. We'd fight until dawn with Alberto watching over me. He'd only step in when I was on the brink of being taken down; when I only had two or three breaths left before passing out. He really put me through it. What I had was a genuine, traditional apprenticeship. And I was willing to give my life for it from the beginning. Which is why I learned much faster than most.

"More recently, Alberto worked with Don Julio Llerena Pinedo, another master shaman. I asked Julio if he'd teach me too. But he was in his late eighties and told me 'no' at first, saying he was too old, that taking on an apprentice at his age could kill him.

"He lived just 400 metres from my house, and one day I heard him screaming in terrible pain. Alberto was back in Herrera. Since there was nobody else around, I grabbed my shacapa and tobacco and went to see if I could help. When I got there Julio's right leg was purple and swollen three times its normal size. It seemed as if an invisible force was trying to break his ankle. He told me that he'd been hit by witchcraft. I had no formal training in this kind of situation, but I knew instinctively what to do. I started sucking on his leg. And when I did, I spat out blood even though the skin wasn't broken. After working on him for a few minutes, the swelling went down, and his leg was back to its normal colour.

"'How much do I owe you?' Julio asked me.

"I told him I didn't want any money, but I wanted him to grant me the same honour that he'd given Alberto when he healed Julio from witchcraft years earlier: I wanted him to become my grandfather maestro and teach me the medicine.

"He agreed, and for the next year and ten months my apprenticeship continued at breakneck speed. I lived on a razor's edge of insanity the whole time, as the spirits broke down all the structures I held about myself and life and completely rebuilt my energetic body. All of the teachings came directly from the spirits. Julio and Alberto acted just as guides. The only advice Alberto ever gave me was, 'Drink your ayahuasca and then forget you ever drank it,' and Julio's one piece of wisdom, 'Drink your ayahuasca, blow smoke on your chest three times, and in the morning bathe in the river.' That was it!

"By the end of that time, not even two years later, I healed my physical body from the witchcraft attacks and was given the title of *maestro*—master shaman—the highest rank in our lineage.

"During that period we had a few people on each tour and news of our camp was beginning to spread. But it wasn't until three years after starting Blue Morpho that I finally made a monthly profit. The logistics of getting ten or twelve guests out to the old camp, together with all the necessary supplies, was complicated and time-consuming. By early 2005, I realised I no longer needed to be in such a remote location. So I started looking for land that was more accessible from Iquitos. Then I found the plot we're sitting on today.

"We began constructing the new camp immediately. Within a couple of months we had a new road, water and sewage systems and three main buildings, just in time for our first tour. Since then, we've continued to expand."

Despite the horrific circumstances that brought me here, I feel fortunate to get to spend time with this extraordinary human being. I vow that if he can do all that, then I can heal myself. I will not let him or myself down.

* * *

As I make my way across the newly laid brick path that now connects all buildings, I look up at the night sky, glimmering with millions of stars, each a beacon of light filling my heart with hope. The Milky Way streaks across the centre, so close I can almost touch it.

I enter the ceremonial house and head to the right of the apprentices' seats where a blue, plastic chair is placed. This will be my spot for all ceremonies from now on. Hamilton told me that moving from a mattress to a chair will help me manage my ceremonies more effectively.

Unfortunately, I soon discover that the simple act of sitting up straight makes the intensity of the *mareación*—the overall effects of the ayahuasca—much stronger. I'm hit with such a force that I find myself slumped with my head on my knees, fighting to stay in the chair.

Suddenly, I hear a voice in my head, "Sit up," it says. "Sit up."

After a moment, I realise that for the very first time I'm hearing the medicine spirits, *Oh my God, oh my God, the spirits are talking to me*, I think as my heart pounds against my ribcage, and sweat drips into my eyes.

"We are here to help you. Trust us," they say. "Wouldn't you rather be talking with us than those demonic entities that you've been communing with all your life—those that bring you dark thoughts, confusion and fear?" They have a point.

I make a half-hearted effort to sit up, but it takes so much strength to remain upright that I'm soon horizontal once more. Immediately, I hear them again, "Sit up."

They are gentle, kind and insistent. They do not stop until I'm again in the desired position. This goes on all night long. I'm never able to sit up for more than a couple of minutes. I must resemble a drunk on the night bus home, locked in a constant cycle of slumping and jerking upright. However, ridiculous I may look, this simple effort is making me stronger.

Simultaneously, I fight a stream of dark entities. One after another they appear, each with an associated vision. I see witches that entered me after taking Ecstasy at a festival in Portugal, spirits of self-hatred, and demons related to the witchcraft in Africa. I am resolute. Despite the severe nausea and fatigue that these apparitions produce, I almost enjoy the tussle as one by one I purge them from my body, releasing them back into the Infinite.

One moment I'm on the toilet in a jungle lodge in the Amazon, the next I'm back at the Solipse festival in Zambia, witnessing myself walking towards the bar, seeing myself step on the talisman of animal hairs. In a blinding flash, wicked beings of misery and suffering cascade out of it and enter my body through my foot. I watch as they set up home inside me, the presence of their energy slowly but surely taking over my body, moving deeper and deeper into the essence of my being, causing illness to develop and spread while they poison my mind with their negativity.

And then the spirit of a young man appears in front of me. He is in his mid-twenties, with long, black hair tied back in a ponytail. I know instinctively that he is English.

"I've come to apologise," he says. "I was given that talisman by a local man I met there in Africa. I had no idea what it was or that he was a witchdoctor. It was in my pocket that night at the festival and must have fallen onto the ground at some point. I'm so sorry."

"It's not a problem," I reply. "I don't blame you for anything that's happened."

It's true, I don't. I understand the darkness I was already carrying in my soul somehow attracted this malevolence. The witchdoctor involved hadn't intended for me to be the recipient of the evil.

Later the same week, the witchdoctor himself shows up in ceremony, confirming my assumption. Rather than threaten me, he merely watches. I call out to Hamilton who tells me he's come for his *materials*. In the shamanic world, materials are spiritual tools that have the power to harm or heal depending on how they are used. When I stepped on the talisman some of his materials entered my body.

Suddenly a wave of nausea hits me so hard I'm barely able to grab my bucket in time. I throw up violently several times before the feeling leaves me as quickly as it arrived. Hamilton tells me that he removed the materials and certainly isn't going to give them back to the witchdoctor.

"If he wants them he can come and fight me," Hamilton says. The witchdoctor must have thought better of it since he leaves and never returns.

SHEDDING THE LAYERS

* * *

By the middle of June, four months after arriving back at Blue Morpho, I'm at last well enough to be drinking in every ceremony. My skin is no longer falling off in such large quantities. The oozing only occurs during and after ceremony. Moving around still causes some pain, but as long as I don't do too much, I don't need painkillers or antihistamines.

While positive external changes are taking place, that's not the case on the inside. The numerous ceremonies and shamanic diets have really shaken me up. My emotions are all over the place. Even when I'm not in ceremony, out of nowhere I'll feel terrified, sad or overwhelmed. I'm being opened up, and I'm not at all sure that I like it. The world has suddenly become a much bigger place. My head cannot come to terms with the scale of it.

My whole idea of life, of what it is and how it works, is changing rapidly. This physical world that our bodies inhabit, that until recently I was convinced was the totality of everything, is no more than the tiniest fraction of what is really out there. My mind cannot comprehend what my experience is telling me. It goes spinning off into a world of panic and confusion until I'm able to focus on a mundane task that brings me back into this world of form.

Over and over again I question, *Why is this happening to me? I'm not ready for all this information. It's too much. I can't handle it.* It is all I can do to hang on and not go crazy. All I ever wanted was a quiet, stress-free life.

If that isn't enough, I still can't let go of the fear that I'm going to have to become an ayahuasca shaman. The only thing worse would be living with the physical illness forever. As terrifying as the idea of being a shaman is, it's more appealing than the alternative.

But only slightly.

Every time the effects of the ayahuasca start to come on, I believe this will be the time it will be revealed. Every night I ask the spirits, and every time they patiently answer me in the same way, "No, you do not have to become an ayahuasca shaman."

"Life doesn't work like that," Mimi explains to me one afternoon as we relax in rocking chairs in the apprentices' bungalow. "When you find what it is that you're meant to do, it'll be exactly what you want to do; it'll be perfect, and you'll love doing it."

Mimi is in her early thirties, of Sicilian descent, born and raised in south London. With the dark features of her heritage, she has a smouldering beauty. She smiles, and I feel instantly at ease.

"That sounds nice in theory," I reply, "but I just don't believe it. It seems too good to be true."

"You still have a lot of dark spirits in you that stop you from seeing the truth," she continues. "Once you get rid of them you'll understand how beautiful and amazing life really is. It's the ultimate gift. I used to lack belief too. The ayahuasca showed me it was because of my low self-esteem. Once I purged that negativity the whole world changed."

By her own admission, Mimi had something of a wild youth, attending school only very occasionally after getting thrown out of most classes for disruptive behaviour. She left with virtually no qualifications but later trained as a nurse before heading to South America, having always had the feeling that she would visit for an extended period of time. She came across ayahuasca while trying to find somebody to teach her about natural plant medicine. After a horrific first experience—not helped by her drinking a few beers beforehand to calm her nerves—Mimi wanted nothing more to do with it. Then, she ended up stuck, sick, in Iquitos.

"I felt like I was so close to finding what I'd been looking for," she told me previously, "and yet it was just out of my grasp. I was in a terrible emotional state. I called my sister in tears. She told me to calm down and just stay put, not to go anywhere. Shortly afterwards I met Hamilton."

Together, they went out to the old Blue Morpho camp to do a diet without Mimi knowing what it really entailed.

"Hamilton explained the process to me on the ferry to the camp. When he started talking about putting tree spirits into my body I panicked. But then I looked at him, and I just knew he was for real. It was as if I was hearing the truth for the very first time, and I thought *what the hell, I'm already on my way, so let's just get on with it.*"

That was back in April 2005 and Mimi has been here ever since. She's a real source of inspiration and strength. I've witnessed her go through a torrid time for months, both inside and outside of ceremony. She cries almost daily, must run off into the jungle to scream and shout to release her anger and resentment, and has days when she's convinced she's going insane, her whole world disintegrating around her. Yet through it all she remains determined and dedicated to her apprenticeship. And her hard work is starting to pay off. She is transforming into a different person. Rather, she is becoming more herself—happier, more confident and stronger. When things get tough I think of Mimi, which reminds me that I can do it, that anything is possible if I'm prepared to work hard enough.

"Ayahuasca doesn't make life any easier," she tells me. "If anything, it gets harder. But so much better at the same time. I love this life even though it kicks my arse all the time. I wouldn't swap it for anything.

"The beauty about ayahuasca," she adds, "is the strength you find in the really tough moments in ceremony—when it seems too hard, but you find a way through—that strength stays with you forever. You earn it. It's yours. Then, a situation that in the past would have made you angry or sad or scared doesn't have the same effect on you anymore. It's so much easier to deal with."

* * *

The spirits tell me that I must see this healing through to the end. And I vow to do just that. From the very start I've been committed to doing whatever it takes. I'm not going to quit now. I have no idea how my life will be once all this is over. Yet I have no choice but to keep taking that next step forward and to trust as much as possible that all is happening for the best. The spirits also tell me that I will love my life, and it will contain everything I've ever wanted. In spite of my doubts, it's enough to help me onwards.

To help speed my recovery along, every ceremony without fail Hamilton comes over to where I'm sitting and, together with his apprentices, gives me a venteada. As they begin to sing, the intensity of the ayahuasca is cranked right up—the energies of the icaros are all around me, swirling patterns in technicolor that I'm not so much seeing as I am a part of, merging with my being so I cannot tell where I end and they begin. I sense them searching my entire body for anything that has to be removed, delving into those long-forgotten corners that I don't want to revisit.

My stomach lurches. I bend over and deposit an explosive stream of negative emotions into my bucket.

"Wow," says the petite Russian girl next to me. "You fart like a girl, but you puke like a MAN!"

* * *

For the best part of eighteen months, my days have been spent moving as little as possible. Which has been tough given that I'm someone for whom exercise was an important part of life. Now that I have finally regained almost full flexibility in my arms and legs, I can start getting back into shape. After each exercise, the excessive heat from the illness transfers to the surface of my skin, making it inflamed and itchy. I have to sit in front of the fan for a few minutes to cool off. Fortunately, by morning all has calmed back down.

Despite the discomfort, I build up to a ninety-minute routine. A few weeks later, my super-skinny frame finally starts to get some of its muscle definition back. It's been so long since I've woken up with aching muscles. It's a wonderful sensation, helping me to finally begin feeling human again. The skin on my arms and chest is even closer to its normal colour.

Sleeping is still very difficult. I often lie awake until 4 or 5 a.m. I can feel the poison inside me, running through my nerves and clogging my bones. A deep, persistent ache emanates from my nervous system that makes it impossible for me to remain in the same position for more than a few minutes. The lymph nodes in my neck, armpits and groin are as swollen as ever, and I still have very little hair on my body.

September is approaching and with it, a break in the schedule. Now that my recovery is in full swing, it's a good opportunity to head home, visit friends and family and earn some money. I book a flight that gets me back to England on my birthday. The prospect of cool weather excites me. I look forward to walking in the park, running and cycling.

Until then, the ceremonies continue unabated. Now, I am less afraid as I wait for my turn to drink because I have more trust in my ability to stay positive throughout the experience. In daily life,

I'm also calmer and less likely to get annoyed or upset when I'm challenged by the unexpected.

Furthermore, I feel much freer to be myself. People notice this shift and want to be around me more. My positivity is even rubbing off on them. While I wouldn't wish what happened to me on anybody, this experience has sparked a vital transformation. With the physical pain finally behind me, I know complete health cannot be far away.

Even though I've been at Blue Morpho just over seven months, it feels like a lifetime, maybe two. The trip home is still uncomfortable, but nothing compared to getting here. I'm proud of how far I've come. After not having worked for over two and a half years the thought of having a normal life again excites me, even doing mundane office work.

However, if I had known what was going to happen during my time back home, I would certainly have never returned.

CHAPTER 8
A Well-Earned Holiday

As the plane approaches Heathrow it is evident that we'll have to join the obligatory queue of planes circling the London skies. We continue eastwards past the airport and over West London towards the city centre. The sun is setting. There's not a cloud in the crystalline-blue sky. As we follow the course of the River Thames I can make out Ealing, where I used to live, followed by all the famous landmarks: Hyde Park, the Houses of Parliament and Big Ben, the Millennium Wheel and St Paul's Cathedral. We fly past Canary Wharf, out to the Thames Barrier in the east. Then the pilot turns the plane round, and I get to see it all from the opposite direction, picking out places I used to go and remembering the good times I had living in this captivating city. I am home.

I meet my parents in Arrivals. My mom coos about how much better I look. By the time we're back in Walsall it's evening. It doesn't bother me in the least that I've spent most of my birthday travelling. Now that I'm back to being a normal person, every day is precious. The next day I go in search of work. After visiting a couple of agencies that specialise in temporary office work, I'm offered a job starting in a few days. I don't care what I do as long as I can begin immediately since it'll take four weeks of work just to pay off my credit card bill for the flight home.

At the weekend I go to Wales with my parents and niece. Even though my parents bought a mobile home on the edge of Snowdonia National Park a couple years ago, I haven't been well enough to visit until now. Compared to the caravans of my childhood, this one is a palace. Carpeted throughout, with a fully furnished kitchen, lounge with settees and dining table, two bedrooms and a bathroom, I could quite happily live here.

We spend Saturday on the beach, a glorious day for late-September Britain. Despite my best efforts at keeping out of the sun, I wind up getting burnt. I spent more than half a year in temperatures over 30°C with no problem, yet fail to negotiate one autumn afternoon in Wales.

The following day we hang out at the campsite, searching unsuccessfully for water buffalo and birdwatching in one of the hides close to a small lake. I cherish the time I spend with my niece, a genuine, open girl with an inexhaustible supply of energy, always ready for the next game, story or activity. How her parents keep up with her I do not know. After a few hours I'm flagging and have to tag my mom in to take over.

My re-entry to working life is slow, I must wait for the IT department to set up my log on details. In the meantime, all my boss can offer me is a stack of company manuals to read. They're irrelevant and mind-numbingly boring, so I spend the entire day drifting in and out of consciousness.

By the next morning, I have my own desk and computer and am able to start actually working. It comes as no surprise that the job is monotonous—mostly data entry. Unlike the temporary positions I've had in the past, I at least get to make some decisions for myself and have to phone other companies from time to time. I can easily handle this for the next six weeks. Plus, with the option to work overtime, I'll be able to earn more money than expected.

At the weekend I travel down to Surrey for a housewarming where the alcohol is flowing freely. Fortunately, I don't feel the slightest desire to drink. I'm having plenty of fun catching up on gossip with old friends.

As relaxed as I may feel, I'm still very much aware my difficulties getting around. I thought that once out of the heat and humidity of the jungle, my movement wouldn't be as restricted. Even back in temperate Britain, my skin starts to itch as a result of simply getting out of a chair. Even at the party, I must remain motionless whenever possible, which having become second nature, doesn't stop me from thoroughly enjoying my evening.

By my second week at work my face is markedly redder. My arms are getting worse. I have to abandon my lunchtime walks, as it's become too painful. Even the short walk across the office to the drinks machine is a struggle. I start to keep my moisturising cream in one of my desk drawers and need to use it more and more frequently. Before long, I can't use the keyboard unless my arms are completely covered with cream. Every day I long to get home, strip naked and slather my entire body with it.

I can't spend the following weekend in London as planned. Instead, I can only manage a few hours on Sunday to meet up with my good friend Cordelia. Alluring and passionate with unruly brown hair and a smile that makes me feel like everything's right with the world, Cords greets me with a big hug. We eat lunch at a little cafe on Baker Street where we chat for hours. Ever since I've known Cords she has been confronting problems and pushing herself to do things that she finds demanding. Now she's close to qualifying as an Art Therapist, a course which has tested her more than anything else.

"You know, I used to wonder why you made life so hard for yourself," I say, wagging my chicken baguette in her direction. "Why you made yourself permanently stressed. I was always so different, forever choosing the easy option in life, avoiding any sort of confrontation or challenge. I couldn't understand anyone who didn't do the same."

"And now?" she asks.

"Now I get it. The ayahuasca has shown me that it's precisely these tough situations that make you grow, that help you become the person you've always wanted to be. Challenges are the very essence of life. The people who say, 'Yes' to all of them are really living. As much as life can knock you down, you have to get up and do it all over again. Only when you've come through a demanding time can you see how much you've grown and only then, can you understand and be grateful for the experience."

"You know, you've really changed! I'm so pleased for you," she says smiling. "You look so much happier."

"It's really very simple: follow the path of your heart, and you'll be fulfilled. That's it. Simple, but not at all easy," I conclude with a grin.

Cords is a person who leads with her heart, which is why I love being in her company. I can't help but regret that my intimacy issues prevented me from having a romantic relationship with her years ago.

The conversation flows as we discuss our lives. It's hard to believe that we last saw each other over a year and a half ago. Back then, I sat in her flat excitedly relating my first trip to Blue Morpho from which I'd just returned, unaware that my whole world was about to fall apart.

It's time for me to leave for my train way too soon. After we say our goodbyes, I head for the station, my body stiffening more and more as the minutes pass. By the time the train pulls into dark and dreary Walsall, my skin aches.

At the end of the following workday, I'm once again in agony. I go to bed straight after dinner. By Tuesday, my arms hurt so much I can't focus on doing any work. Even if I could, I wouldn't be able to hold them in the necessary position to type. At lunchtime, I explain the situation to my boss and leave, knowing I won't return, after just ten and a half days of work.

When I return home, the sight of me brings my mom to tears. I can't help but feel the old pangs of guilt.

* * *

The following weeks assume a familiar pattern as I spend long days in my room watching TV. At least the pain isn't as bad as last year. As long as I don't go anywhere or do anything I'm okay. Now all I can do is wait out the next month until it's time to return to Peru.

My financial predicament forces me to ask my parents for a loan. As much as they may want me to stay and doubt the efficacy of the treatment, they give me the money. Full of gratitude, I think about how they will rejoice once this nightmare is over, how they'll be delighted to see the person I've become. The physical transformation will be a reflection of the internal changes that continue to take place. I'm determined to become the loving, caring, open and honest son I've never been able to be.

* * *

Over the last few years I've become a master of idly passing time. So the days leading up to my flight evaporate quickly. With a week to go, there is just one task I must do: I have to start using the steroid cream. It's the only thing that can suppress the eczema enough to make it back to Iquitos.

However anxious I may be about having to go without it once I'm there, I remain confident that whatever happens won't be as bad as last time. The cream is a necessary evil. I apply it to my arms, legs and face, using the smallest amount necessary in an attempt to minimise the flare-up that will follow its suspension of use.

A few days later, red blotches cover my chest and back. Working hard to quell the rising anxiety, I begin using the cream all over. With only one day to go, I smother my entire body in the strongest cream.

SHEDDING THE LAYERS

Once I'm in Peru I'm prepared to accept whatever physical suffering results. But first, I have to get there.

While I lie in bed the night prior to my departure, fear and misery begin to creep up again, pulling at my soul with their gnarled fingers, intent on dragging me back down into my old existence. I fight them off as best I can, knowing that in 36 short hours I will be back in the jungle.

The beeping of my alarm clock rouses me from an agitated sleep. As I reach to turn it off, the skin on my arm rips. My eyes brim with tears. My whole being fills with terror. In the faint light of the full moon I can see that my chest and arms are covered in eczema. I stumble to the bathroom to survey the damage. My entire body is in the same state. I stare into the mirror at the grotesque image facing me.

"Come on Mark," I tell my reflection. "You can do this. Get strong, stop thinking and get going."

But this time I know that I really can't. Petrified by the thought, I look myself in the eye.

"Either you get on that plane," I say, "or you commit suicide. Those are the options. The only options."

I say this as a fact, not a threat. There is no alternative. Another forty years or more like this, never leaving the house, just waiting to die is absolutely not an option. As I continue to look deep into my forlorn eyes, the answer is clear: I cannot travel. Suddenly, all my strength evaporates. I collapse on the floor.

CHAPTER 9
Dark Night of the Soul

I lurch out of the bathroom and bump into my mom.

"I'm not going," I tell her. She doesn't need to ask why. My dad is already up, ready to take me to the airport. He's undoubtedly relieved to hear the news, glad that I've finally seen sense.

"Have you cancelled your flight so you can get your money back?" he asks. I hadn't even thought about it. At this hour, my only option is going to the airport, and I'm not even sure they'll give me a refund. Nonetheless, I take my dad up on his offer to drive me there. It's a small price to pay to avoid an inevitable argument about potentially losing the money.

We spend the forty-five minute trip in total silence. While I wait for the information desk to open, I stare blankly at the passengers checking in for the flight I was meant to be on. The desk finally opens. I cancel my ticket, go home and get straight back in bed.

Once awake, I question the point of getting up. Now that I can't travel, I have no purpose, no hope.

Eventually, of course, I must move. On autopilot, I call the local private hospital and arrange an appointment with Dr. Basu. I request a course of the immunosuppressant drug ciclosporin that we'd discussed previously. Even if I'm powerless over the emotional devastation, at least there's a chance of easing the physical pain.

In his office, I break down completely, crying properly for the first time in many years. As much as I need a good long weep, I'm ashamed of myself and quickly stem the flow of tears. Ciclosporin is a potent drug, which works by damping down the immune system. Typically, transplant patients take it to prevent their bodies from rejecting the new organ. It can also be used for a short duration in cases of severe eczema.

I'd long rejected the idea of taking it due to the possible side effects—kidney problems, high blood pressure, seizures, partial paralysis, blindness and coma—to name just a few. Now, even a brief respite from the immediate suffering far outweighs the long-term damage to my body. I won't be around long enough for it to matter anyway.

Prescription in hand, I return home to the solitude of my bedroom. My packed rucksack lies forsaken in the middle of the floor. I step over it and curl up on my bed.

* * *

In the morning, I lie still for hours, watching the same thought swirl around in my mind: *How did my life end up like this?* There's no answer.

I was so sure the ayahuasca was working; that it would heal me, given enough time. In the jungle I learnt that there is meaning behind everything that happens in life. There must be a reason why I discovered the vine. It's inconceivable that I would be taken part-way through my healing and then just abandoned. Yet here I am. I had so much to give, had learnt so much from this experience that I wanted to share with the world. But that opportunity has been denied me. All that remains is for me to take my own life. I glare at my untouched rucksack across the room.

Now, the reason I exist is only to consider options for suicide. I can't bring myself to go for a fool-proof approach such as throwing myself in front of a train or jumping off a building—too public with a potentially large impact on other lives. Slashing my wrists is a possibility. Then again, it would be cruel to leave my parents to find me in a pool of blood. It will have a lesser impact on them if my body isn't disfigured. I also rule out carbon monoxide poisoning because I would have to use their car. Finally, I decide on a concoction of tablets.

One major problem with my chosen method still remains: my parents will be the ones who discover the body. I can see no way around this. I will be killing not just myself, but the two people I love more than anything in the world. But what choice do I have?

At the chemist's, I buy some paracetamol to complement the pills I already have in the house: antihistamines, codeine and ciclosporin. To prevent any chance of my survival, I must take as many tablets as possible.

Even though I now know, without any shadow of doubt, that life does not end with death, and I'll still have to face whatever issues are behind my illness, I'd rather take my chances in the spirit world.

I draw up a list of all the people I would like to be told of my death, together with their contact details. I plan what readings I want at my funeral—a poem by Ben Okri, *To An English Friend In Africa* and a passage about death from *The Prophet* by Khalil Gibran.

I consider what I would like to say in a note to my friends and of course, my dear parents. I will hurt so many people. I find myself heaping a ton of guilt on top of my already unbearable burden. Still, death remains preferable to the life that the future holds for me.

My mind continues to churn as I try to reconcile what I've learnt through ayahuasca with my current situation. I know that in life there is a purpose to all things, and that I need to trust in the higher power of the Universe. I know that I'm not my body. I know that my Divine Self is untouched by my physical pain and suffering. I know all this intellectually, but it counts for nothing, as I cannot *feel* it.

All I can think is *Why? Why has God turned his back on me? Where is my reward for all I have endured and survived?* I gather the pills together in a pile and imagine swallowing them by the handful, then lying down for the final time. I fantasise about the blissful ignorance that death will bring. Yet no matter how hard I try to reason that this is the only sensible option, a force deep within me simply will not allow it. As illogical as it may seem to me in the moment, I cannot deny this knowing, a sense that for whatever reason, I'm meant to live. I put the pills back in the drawer.

* * *

Winter exposes the bare branches of the tree outside my window. Night arrives earlier and stays later, as the grass becomes covered in a silvery coating of frost. It takes me three weeks to get round to unpacking my rucksack, my heart heavy as the clothes go back in the wardrobe. I'm reminded of the teachings of ayahuasca and how the tough times are there for a reason, to help me grow. If that's true I reckon I'll be twelve feet tall by the time this is all over.

On the final day of the year I go to bed early and fall into an unusually deep sleep. I awake disorientated to find that I'm no longer in my bed. Several pairs of eyes peer down at me. I cannot see their forms but feel their essence and know they're benevolent and compassionate. They are the medicine spirits. "We are with you, Mark, now and always. All you have to do is call on us and we will help you." A caressing, golden light fills my being. I wake up again, this time back in my bed.

I'm definitely awake now, but I can still hear the spirits. I'd be petrified, except that everything they say is positive and loving. "You will return to Peru," they tell me. "Everything will work out perfectly. You will heal yourself completely and you will love your life." An unbidden flicker of hope returns.

I recall what Hamilton said about shamanic diets and why it's a process that must not be taken lightly. "By participating in a diet you're inviting the medicine spirits of the dieted plants into your body," he told us. "Then, they live inside of you forever and make changes that will continue for the rest of your life. The spirits literally move from living inside a tree in the Amazon jungle to living in your body. They accompany you everywhere, always. To diet is to make a serious commitment to change."

Every day now I communicate with the spirits. I hear them as thoughts in my head, in my own voice. Their tone is softer and quieter than the other thoughts. Yet their words are spoken with a clarity and authority that pierces all doubt. They insist that I'll find happiness even though they don't tell me anything specific about the future. That's enough for me. It is all I've ever wanted.

Whenever I get depressed and want to feel sorry for myself, which is often, the spirits appear, reminding me of everything I have in my life. They teach me the importance of gratitude. "You already have more than enough to be you. You already are perfect. You just don't think you are," they tell me.

I sense them slowly but surely retraining my mind to start thinking positively. Previously I was ignorant of how negative my thought patterns were. Now, every time I have such a thought, the spirits immediately tell me not to be fooled, that there's no truth in it. Soon, even without their prompting, I begin to replace negative thoughts with positive. Much of the time I don't really believe it. Nevertheless I persist, as I know it's a step in the right direction.

Following what the spirits told me, I check the 2007 schedule on the Blue Morpho website. There are only two workshops between now and May, so there's no point in returning before then. In spite of the relapse, I'm sure my health is better than it was six months ago, and I'm prepared to go back and do it all again, no matter how long it takes.

For the sake of my sanity, I cannot sit around the house for another five months. Thanks to the immunosuppressants and a twice-daily generous application of steroid cream, I'm now able to wear clothes and walk around in relative comfort. The cream should only be used for a maximum of two weeks, as it causes thinning of the skin, and the tablets, two months due to their long list of side effects. However, I have a big stash of cream and convince Dr. Basu to let me take the pills until May.

I find a job answering telephones for an insurance company. The pay is decent for temp work. That is all that matters. Some days the itching of my skin doesn't relent for hours. I scream inside my head to prevent me from screaming aloud.

It's not long before the work helps me to appreciate the changes that have taken place within me. All day long I speak with unhappy customers who have legitimate complaints about the terrible service they are receiving. They are often angry and shout at, or even insult, me. In the past, I hated any sort of confrontation and would have quickly become frustrated, been rude to the customers and quit within a couple of days.

Now, I'm able to witness the tension as it starts to build inside me. Rather than react on impulse, I'm an impartial observer. I watch calmly as "Mark" deals with the call, which usually has a positive impact on the caller's behaviour. If I remain kind and courteous they calm down, and we're able to have a constructive conversation. Sometimes they even apologise for their conduct.

It occurs to me that when I get annoyed, it's the anger within me that prompts it, not what's currently happening. The present situation is simply pushing on my own stuff and out comes the irritation as a knee-jerk reaction without any conscious thought. Having purged a large amount of darkness during the ayahuasca ceremonies, that reflex is no longer there. More often than not I'm able to stay present and not let the negativity affect me.

However taxing the work may be, I start to see everything as a challenge rather than a problem (an idea I used to scoff at). Worse than all of the rude customers is Melanie, one of the loss assessors for whom I answer the phone. She is one of the angriest people I've ever met. Against company policy she invariably tries to make me deal with calls from her clients. She knows they will be upset with her because she has done no work on their claims.

Looming five inches taller than me, Melanie operates by intimidation and bullying. When she refuses to take my call and ignores my shout across the office, I walk up to her desk.

"There's a client on the phone for you," I say in my most polite voice.

"Oh, for fuck's sake. Take a message," she barks in what could actually be her most polite voice.

"He insists on speaking to you now. He says he's been leaving messages for the last two weeks and you haven't got back to him."

"Did you not hear what I just fucking said? TAKE A MESSAGE. I'm busy."

She's so angry I'm surprised she doesn't spontaneously combust. The verbal assault leaves me shaking on the inside. Melanie's boss overhears the commotion and call us into her office. I explain what happened with only a slight wobble in my voice. She makes Melanie apologise to me.

Previously, this whole episode would have reduced me to a tongue-tied, quivering mess. I realise how perfect this job is for me at this present moment, feeling a strong sense of the spirits' influence. I've been guided here in order both to grow and witness just how far I've come.

As the weeks pass I settle into a routine. My working day is longer than I've ever been used to. With a lengthy commute I'm out of the house for eleven hours each day. Initially this makes me resentful, but the irritation disappears when I consider that I wouldn't be doing anything except watching TV or surfing the internet anyway. As opposed to the old Mark who railed against the unfairness of reality, I no longer waste energy fighting against what simply is.

* * *

Sitting on the bus home after a hard day's work, I experience moments of contentment and peace watching the comings and goings of society. When I really take the time to stop and look, there is nothing more fascinating than human beings—from the shaven-headed, *Sun*-reading postal worker with tattooed arms thicker than my legs to the immaculately dressed young blind man being guided to his seat by a kindly office worker.

With a calm mind, even a bus ride through dark and rainy Birmingham can be a pleasurable experience. Yet the conflict and the negative thoughts are never too far away: *How can you be happy, knowing what pain and suffering awaits you when you return to Peru?* The good feelings immediately vanish, replaced with trepidation.

I've feared that I'll only be happy once I'm one hundred percent healthy. Now, I'm no longer fooled into thinking that true happiness lies at some mysterious point in the future. Joy cannot exist in any moment other than the present. Discovering happiness and love in my life right now is what will actually heal me. Finally, I'm also starting to see through the illusion of my desire for external gratification. I'll never find fulfilment by looking outside myself. I must turn within for what I seek.

Looking at my past behaviours, almost everything I ever did

was a way of avoiding myself, distracting myself from the emotions I feared would overwhelm me. The stronger I feel about confronting those emotions, the more faith I have in my ability to find peace.

When I consider the profundity of the changes that are taking place within me, I have to laugh at the futility of thinking about it. This is so far beyond my comprehension that trying to work it out only brings confusion and despair. If I'm not careful, when I look at the possibilities of human existence, of *my* existence, I'll also see how far I am from achieving my potential. I will become impatient, wanting to arrive at the destination without the work. I'll want to instantly feel the ecstasy and peace that are waiting there for me. But I must keep reminding myself that these wonderful feelings are created *by* the struggle. It *has* to be this difficult, has to be almost impossible, for the rewards to be so great.

I must bless all my sufferings, as it is precisely the effort involved in overcoming them that will lead to joy. I make a commitment to myself to say *YES*. Yes to the pain. Yes to the fear. Yes to the illness. Yes to my life exactly as it is. I accept all my challenges and commit once more to doing whatever it takes to free myself from this disease. Now I actually feel fortunate. I wasn't given the option of continuing to live a life that was tolerably unsatisfactory. I was given the gift of losing everything, of reaching a point where I would rather have died than continue with my life the way it was.

I place my faith in the Universe. I trust that I'll be guided in this discovery of my reason for being. As long as I keep taking the next step, I know I'll be provided with everything I need. Only by discarding layer after layer of that which no longer serves will I uncover who I really am.

I feel a surge of power and courage shoot through my body.

* * *

In late April I book my flight back to Peru. This time I buy a one-way ticket. My parents' reactions are as expected: My dad says nothing. My mom is clearly upset but accepting.

"If there was any other way to heal myself I would take it," I tell them, "but for whatever reason it has to be this way."

"I don't blame you," my mom says. "The only thing that matters is that you get better, and if you think this will work then you have to do it."

As departure day approaches, I consider what is to come. My mind is my greatest tool, so I keep the stream of positive thoughts open. Looking back on the previous twenty-eight months, the fact that I'm still alive is nothing short of a miracle. If I can come this far, I can do anything.

One crisp Spring morning I head to Birmingham Airport, not knowing when I'll be home again.

CHAPTER 10
Following the Call of the Medicine

As the bus winds down the mud pit that is the road to camp, the exhilaration of being back and having the chance to save my life mixes with anxiety about what I must confront in the coming months, possibly years.

We pass a brand new building, a meditation and arts and crafts centre built on the edge of the lake—a place I've never been able to visit despite it being only one hundred yards from the main camp.

The flowers and shrubs planted last year now stretch six feet into the sky, flooding the area with colour. Down the slope beyond the ayahuasca cookhouse, four guest bungalows stand side by side, each containing six individual rooms. New trails lead off into the jungle beyond the camp. For now they'll remain nothing more than lines drawn on a map to me. My bed, the dining table and the ceremonial house will be the only places of interest.

Tonight, the jungle is unusually quiet, as though preparing itself for the onslaught of the upcoming ceremony. I stopped taking the immunosuppressants yesterday, and the steroid cream will be off-limits as soon as I drink. When Don Alberto and Hamilton enter the room and get down to the business of preparing our plant drink, a hush falls over the group. I push away the legions of dark thoughts ready to storm their way into my consciousness. I ask the spirits for all the help in the world. A cup is passed to me. I down it in one swift movement. The haunting sound of the icaros brings back jolting memories of the previous year.

I fall out of my chair, smacking my body against the hard wood floor. I'm a rag doll at the mercy of a force much greater than me. My whole body shakes. My arms and legs flail wildly while my head jerks from side to side. I'm left without a single coherent thought. Briefly I become lucid and attempt to calm down, telling myself that insanity is not an option, and my only goal is survival. All I can do is relax my muscles as much as possible and allow the contortions to continue, reminding myself over and over that this *will* end, that nothing bad is actually happening.

I become aware of an immense presence towering over me. I cower in front of this invisible force that I know to be God, begging forgiveness for what I've done to myself, for shutting out love. He tells me that I must release the suffering in my heart. Although I may have faith in my ability to survive these terrifying experiences, confronting what's inside is still too much for me to even consider.

"You give too much power to the darkness," Hamilton tells me the next day. "By focusing the mind and dominating the negative forces you can release it gently, with grace, ease and joy. There's no need for physical distress. Relax and open yourself completely, allow the medicine to remove the crossed energies for you. The more you fight, the harder it will be."

When a big purge happened I always believed that there was little I could do, save hold on and ride it out. If I wasn't mad with pain and fear, the medicine wasn't working. Finally, I'm beginning to believe that maybe, just maybe, healing doesn't have to hurt so much.

* * *

Madlain, a forty-year-old Canadian on her second visit to the Amazon is soft-spoken and frail with sorrowful eyes, set within the innocent face of a child. She was repeatedly raped and sexually abused by her father and a male neighbour between the ages of two and sixteen. After years of unsuccessful therapy, she felt like she couldn't go on living with the anguish of the abuse any longer and came to ayahuasca as her last resort.

She speaks openly about the most atrocious of experiences

without any trace of bitterness or shame, which compels me to be more candid about my own past. Even though I've only known Madlain for a matter of days, I feel closer to her than many of my life-long friends. One afternoon I invite her to my bungalow. While I wait for her to arrive, I struggle to calm my breathing as I think about telling her my darkest secret.

"You're such an inspiration to me that I really feel the need to share something deeply personal," I say, wringing my clammy hands.

"Okay," she replies in an encouraging tone.

"I'm terrified of intimacy and sex," I stammer. "So, I've felt worthless, and I've lived most of my life in fear. What I want most and what scares me most is the same thing—to be in a loving relationship with someone I can share everything."

In spite of wanting to bolt out the door, I stand my ground and continue.

"I never felt like I deserved a girlfriend. So, I could never be myself around women. The only way I ever felt confident enough to sleep with a woman was by getting ridiculously drunk first. It's killing me."

There, I've said it—the most honest a moment I've ever had. I'm trembling inside. My heart lightens. Madlain looks at me with nothing but compassion.

"Thank you for sharing that with me. You're very brave."

"You know, you showed me the true meaning of courage this week," I tell her. "You made me see that I've blown my problems completely out of proportion. Any perceived problem can be overcome with enough effort, resolve and patience. You're an extraordinary woman."

Madlain smiles sweetly.

A lump forms in my throat as I think about her life. I continue,

"Because I've been so shut down, I haven't felt much. I can't remember being genuinely happy since I was a kid. Nor was I ever really depressed until I got sick.

I spent my days just drifting along in a kind of No-Man's-Land."

"I understand completely," Madlain says.

She goes on to tell me a story from her ceremony the other night. She perceived herself as an angelic spirit, witnessing God ask her to go down to Earth to break the chain of sexual abuse that was passed down for centuries until it reached her father.

"Of course I shall," the angel replied. "I work for the light. I'll do whatever you ask of me."

And with that decision, her life path took shape.

* * *

By the end of the first week, I've lost an entire layer of skin from my body, with a second soon to follow. It's time for me to become reacquainted with leaving behind piles of skin, as well as the brown, sticky fluid. Once again, I'm red from head to toe and require painkillers.

As I bemoan my fate, I pull absent-mindedly at the loose skin hanging from the side of my left foot. It tears with sickening ease, leaving half my sole a throbbing patchwork of exposed flesh. Horrified, I try in vain to stick the dangling skin back in place.

Setting foot out of bed is like stepping on hot coals. Through sheer force of will, I make it into ceremony almost every night, sometimes in too much pain to participate much more than drinking a few drops of ayahuasca. What may seem like a token effort to some is a major victory to me.

As if what I'm dealing with isn't enough, there's another

problem: the growing political unrest in Iquitos. One-day strikes are commonplace as groups protest for better pay, more rights, lower fuel costs, etc. Roads are often blockaded with glass and burning tyres, making them impassable. Now there's talk of an indefinite strike during which no boats or flights would be allowed into or out of the city. There are even murmurings of the regional flag of Loreto, of which Iquitos is the capital, being raised in the main square instead of the Peruvian national flag—tantamount to civil war.

Completely reliant on Lima for its goods and supplies, Iquitos only has enough supplies for four days. An indefinite strike would mean that people would starve and anarchy would be inevitable. Earlier Hamilton spoke to town officials who told him that they are almost certain the strike will go ahead. If it does, Hamilton and the apprentices will escape to Lima where they'll stay until the situation is resolved.

Barely able to walk a hundred yards, I'm in a panic. Desperate, I ask the spirits in ceremony if the strike will happen. The answer I receive is "No. It will be called off at the last minute."

How do I really know it's the medicine spirits speaking to me? Could this just be wishful thinking?

In response to my doubts I hear, "Have we ever let you down before? Have we ever been wrong?"

It sounds like the same voices that began to speak to me earlier in the year, the ones that told me I would heal myself. It's hard to trust them since even Hamilton is sure that the strike will take place. All I can do is hope, pray and research hotels in Lima. I steel myself for the journey.

With one day left before the blockade is due to start, I speak with Hamilton. He tells me that the strike has just been called off. "Told you so!" I hear in my head as a knot of tension unwinds in my stomach.

SHEDDING THE LAYERS

* * *

"Why do you think my condition got so much worse after I went home last year?" I ask Hamilton one afternoon as we sit in the main house, listening to the rain pound the leaf roof.

"I'm not entirely sure," he responds, "but what I think probably happened is that through all the venteadas I transferred a tremendous amount of energy to you—my energy. Which helped suppress the symptoms of the condition while the healing continued."

"So the improvements in my health weren't a true representation of my recovery?"

"Exactly. And without continuous venteadas your body wasn't able to hold the increased level of energy. So after a few weeks at home, your skin returned to a condition more accurately reflecting how much illness was still inside it."

I can't help wishing I'd known this before deciding to go home.

* * *

As the ceremonies continue, I feel the spirits pulling the disease out of me. I do my best to resist scratching, sometimes managing an hour, other times barely a minute. Once I start the assault of my skin, it's almost impossible to stop. The more I scratch, the more I itch. Harder and harder I attack my skin, feeling it rip and the blood flow. Even that won't stop me—I must get at the ever-elusive source of the itching deep inside my body. Only once I've done too much damage can I bring myself to take a deep breath and stop to slather the mutilated area with moisturising cream. On contact, it stings like a thousand wasps before it begins to soothe. Almost instantly after caring for myself, I'm compelled to attack another area of my pathetic excuse for a body.

Within a few hours, my T-shirt and trousers are covered in blood. Once the ordeal finally ends, I stumble back to my bungalow where I collapse and plead with the medicine spirits to heal my broken skin quickly, so I can do it all again tomorrow.

This is my life for the next several months. My condition continues to improve, but the progress is heartbreakingly slow. I must accept there's nothing I can do but ride the waves of my emotions and work on surrendering myself to the process.

* * *

Chris returns to Blue Morpho for a short visit in August. Aside from being an apprentice, he's a renowned astrologer and psychic. He's been doing readings for over twenty-five years and owns a successful psychic readers company. With elfin ears and a bald head that comes together in a prominent peak, his distinctive appearance lends him a mysterious edge.

Previously I put aside my scepticism and flipped through one of his astrology books that I came across on the camp bookshelf. I was startled to discover that almost everything he said about Virgo fit me perfectly, right down to the fact that they often contract skin diseases such as eczema.

I'm thrilled when Chris offers to do a Tarot Card reading to obtain more information about my illness. Chris and I have merely been acquaintances over the past year. Only Madlain knows my innermost secrets.

"Focus on the cause of the eczema and then select a card," he tells me.

I do as requested and draw the Fear card, placing it between us on the table.

"Now focus on what the fear is related to and choose two more cards."

I turn over the Strength and Hanged Man cards. Chris pauses to analyse them before speaking,

"The Strength card relates to virility and hence sexuality," he says. "The Hanged Man represents trauma and suppressed pain that has built up over the years because of your fear of sex."

I make my best poker face and say, "Okay."

"Let's look at your recovery now. Select three cards while focusing on the question of how to heal yourself."

I pull out the cards of Courage, Love and The Fool Child. Given that the first two are self-explanatory, Chris tells me that the final card signifies a return to a child-like state of innocence.

"You need to trust that you're cared for by the Universe," he says. "And that everything is going to be okay. You need to relax and play more. Find enjoyment in the little things in life."

I'm astounded that all it took to reveal my biggest fear was flipping over a few cards. I'm not surprised, however, to discover that the illness is related to my intimacy issues. I've read about eczema being related to suppressed emotions. In my case, it's the physical manifestation of my emotional barrier against intimacy. So the witchcraft wasn't the cause; it was the catalyst for my condition.

Later, Chris reads my astrological birth chart. He tells me that my path of recovery will lead to work involving helping others—in a way that involves one-to-one communication.

* * *

As September approaches so does the first break in the schedule, following almost four months of back-to-back tours. Finally well enough to look for my own place to stay, I check out apartments that an English friend of Hamilton's is building on the waterfront. They are undoubtedly the nicest one could find in the whole of Iquitos. The studio apartment is flooded with natural light and comes equipped with air conditioning, cable TV and DVD player, kitchenette and bathroom with hot water—a luxury practically unheard of in Iquitos. Fully furnished with bills included, it costs $200 a month—less than I'm paying for my cramped, windowless hostel room.

I agree at once to take it and head off for the final week at camp. The day I'm finished, the flat will be ready for me to move in. With only six tours scheduled in the next eight months, I'll be spending the majority of my time here. I have no doubt that the medicine spirits were instrumental in my finding this beautiful spot exactly when I needed it.

CHAPTER 11
Struggling with Growth

Much to my relief, the rainy season has arrived, which makes moving around more bearable. When dusk begins to fall, it's cool enough to consider leaving my flat. Below, on the Nanay River to my left, children scamper half-naked outside their floating wooden homes. The sun sets over the water behind them, bathing the air in a hazy orange glow. If it weren't for my stinging feet and legs that demand my full attention I'd stop to take in this majestic scene.

Crossing the Plaza de Armas, the one-legged security guard is poised as usual on his chair outside the chicken restaurant. Grubby shoeshine boys ask to clean my flip-flops. An old woman with a work-hunched body and leathery skin crouches on the ground in front of a set of scales where I can weigh myself for twenty centimos (about 4p / 6c). A scruffy teenage boy draws attention to the little pots of liquid he's selling by sending a cascade of bubbles in my direction. I bat them away in annoyance. He grins.

I walk down Próspero, the main street, a hotchpotch of banks, electrical stores, clothes shops and travel agencies, where I brave the daily assault of money changers thrusting their calculators and wads of cash into my face. Surely by now they know that I'll never stop for them. Here too, copies of the latest films can be bought on the street for five soles (£1 / $1.70) often before they even reach the cinema.

Every few yards I pass another beggar. Outside the bank a man with no legs, always smiling, holds out a plastic cup. A dishevelled old man with twisted limbs and a sign around his neck sprawls across the pavement, forcing me into the road. A blind lady stands with her arm out, muttering under her breath.

Even though it's only five blocks from my flat to the supermarket, I'm exhausted by the time I step inside. The biggest store in town, it's about the same size as an average mini-market. With the greatest speed and economy of movement, I load up with fruit and veg. Many items have seen better days, a product of the isolation of Iquitos.

By the time I finish shopping, darkness has fallen and a faint breeze blows across the waterfront, barely stirring the muggy night air. Amid the pungent aroma of marijuana, bare-chested young men with long dreadlocks and dark, tanned skin sit in front of their displays of homemade jewellery. One guy rides a unicycle whilst another juggles precariously with fire. I'd show them how it's really done if only this useless body of mine would allow it. I used to be something of a master of such skills, having spent countless hours at university honing them while president of the Circus Society.

A large crowd is gathered around a sunken stage where two men are doing slapstick, the throng in uproar as one man kicks his unsuspecting colleague up the backside while he's bending over to tie his shoelace. A smattering of gringos occupies the seats outside the bars and restaurants, sipping cold beer and feasting on freshly caught fish. Iquitos will never be the tourist Mecca that Cusco is. Even so, the *malecón* is lively tonight.

I'm relieved to make it back to the isolation of home where I can be still and let my body recover. I dump the bags on the floor and sink into the welcoming mattress. Ah, the airy freedom of my spacious new flat—no more tiny, windowless, hot and smelly room. And no more worries about the cleaner's reaction to the state of my sheets.

Thank goodness, my body no longer hurts constantly. However, when it does, the discomfort is as bad as ever. Post-shower is the worst time. The minute I turn the water off, my body is on fire again, both inside and out. In these moments I lose all sense of reason. So I shower as infrequently as I can—once during an eight-day workshop when I'm out at camp. That is, until recently when Mimi encouraged me to step it up, "for the benefit of the other guests."

* * *

With the arrival of the new year, my life in 2008 takes a turn for the better. Now able to spend more time in my kitchenette, I develop an interest in cooking. The cuts on my fingers are testament to my lack of experience with a genuinely sharp knife. I cook in short bursts, as standing for more than ten minutes hurts my feet too much. I manage to perfect beef lasagne with garlic and herb baguette. It is real comfort food, a taste of home that cannot be bought in even the best restaurants in town.

Despite my efforts to keep my mind occupied with my new passion, my thoughts always returns to what it knows best—the negative patterns I've lived with my whole life. Like rainwater following erosion gullies in the rocks, it seeks the path of least resistance. Every day I'm assailed by thoughts of giving up. I still can't believe that I will be healed and able to return home.

Exasperated, I ask the spirits, "Will I really be able to do this?"

"Yes," is their simple, insistent reply.

"Then why do I still have so much doubt?"

"Because you don't yet know the truth about life. You must love yourself. You have to work at it, practise, as in any other discipline. Remember, nothing other than the darkness is telling you that you will fail, tricking you into thinking that is your own belief. It is not. Once you stop listening to the dark spirits, they will leave. And when that happens, they will take their negative thought patterns with them, freeing you to revel in the truth that has always been inside you, inside your heart. We can see it. One day you will too. Only then will everything make sense."

* * *

Ceremony after ceremony I search for the truth, for my heart, willing it to open. On this unusually chilly evening, I realise I have no idea how to cultivate self-love, how to feel it. I don't remember ever feeling love in my whole life. There must have been times in my childhood. Right now, however, those memories are unavailable to me.

From the chair to my right Daniel advises me, "Focus on the icaro. Feel it penetrate your heart. Be receptive. Surrender." Then, Chris's voice fills the room:

Pura Pura medicina, Luz divinaini, Luminado Universo, infinitaini
Pura Pura medicina, Luz divinaini, Luminado Universo, infinitaini

Open up your heart to God, courage teaches how
Drink from the fountain of pure joy, dance in the eternal now

Die to your past, again and again, in this way you heal your pain
Die to your past, again and again, in this way you transcend pain

Live each moment fresh and new, let the Universe flow through
Make each moment fresh and new, let the Universe be you

Hold the space for light and dark, purify your divine spark
Hold the space for light and dark, purify your divine spark

Pura Pura medicina, Luz divinaini, Luminado Universo, infinitaini

All I can sense is a wall; the wall I've built around my heart. Made of self-loathing, sadness, loneliness, guilt, shame and fear, there's no budging it.

* * *

"You keep saying that you hate your life. That you don't want to do this. But you *are* doing it. You're still here," Hamilton tells me. "You're a good man Inglés. You don't give yourself enough credit. You're one of the most courageous people I've ever met."

I'm blown away—this coming from someone who's been through so much more than I could imagine. Even more shocking, I'm starting to believe what he's saying. "Thank you. This is such a hard path."

"It is. But it's so worth it. If it weren't, I would've cashed my chips in a long time ago. The day you break through to one moment of true happiness you'll understand that this is *the* most worth-it thing ever. You'll recognise the man that you've become and you'll look back on everything you've been through with genuine gratitude."

So many people at Blue Morpho have given me their help, love, support and friendship. The bond I'm developing with Hamilton, Alberto and the apprentices is stronger than anything I've ever known. After a lifetime of suppressing my feelings, it's a triumph to be able to talk openly without fear of being judged.

* * *

Day follows night, weeks merge into one another, and months slip by as the cycle of relapse and recovery continues. For every three steps forward I take two back. At least I'm making progress.

I while away the daytime hours peeling off the newest layer of flaking skin. How many is that now? Over a thousand I'm sure. As disgusting as it may seem, it's satisfying, as though each time I'm getting one layer closer to being healed, one layer closer to the truth buried beneath my defence mechanisms.

As I peel off the last piece of loose skin on my chest, I have an *a-ha* moment: Focus on love, and I experience love. Focus on fear, and I live in fear. When I shift my awareness elsewhere, to the certainty and security of the present moment, fear ceases to be. It literally does not exist. Since it is my focus that generates all experience, the only thing that ever exists is whatever I place my attention on at any given moment.

Therefore, fear is merely a construct of the mind, born out of a negative anticipation of the future. No matter what my thoughts are telling me, I always have the freedom to choose love or fear; to choose to embrace what's happening right now or be carried away by worries of the future.

A rare smile breaks out across my face as I realise that I don't have to suffer the whims of my moods. I can change them. Until now, whenever I was sad or scared, I passively accepted that was how things were. At last, I see that I have the power to alter my experience in an instant simply by changing my thinking. Instead of wallowing in the suffering, I can focus on joy, happiness and all the wonder in life. By so doing, I am not avoiding the problem, pretending everything is all right when it isn't. Rather, I'm recognising that my life is good, even if it includes "bad" experiences.

In ceremony, a recurring vision of a pretty girl gives me the resolve to battle on. I cannot see her face, but I know she's a redhead. I've always had a penchant for redheads. Her spirit comes and watches me from time to time. I get the impression she is waiting for me to complete this stage of my growth.

* * *

"Hey bro, it's Avi. What you doing next week? I'm coming to Iquitos."

What wonderful news! We've been in the same country for the last year and a half but haven't seen each other once, as I've been too sick to travel and Avi too skint.

"I've got some work with a film crew, so I'm going to be around for a couple of weeks," he happily announces.

He finishes his work the day I return from camp. We spend the next few days hanging out, watching movies and eating a lot of cake and ice cream—sugar being my only remaining vice. Also, I take great pleasure in being able to cook for somebody else, and Avi certainly appreciates it. He has a healthy appetite and a fondness for washing up, which suits me just fine. Even though we don't do much of anything but hang out, actually having a visitor after all my time alone in Iquitos is a momentous event.

"Where do you keep your rubbish?" He calls to me one evening whilst clearing away the debris of a rather fine lentil bolognese.

"In the fridge," I reply with a smile. "Where do you think?"

At this, his eyes widen in cartoon fashion. He laughs so hard he has to hang on to the work surface to stop himself falling over.

"Oh my God. Mark got out of the boat," he says, making reference to a line from the movie "Apocalypse Now" (implying that I've lost my mind).

"Listen mate," I say, eager to defend my actions, "it's the only place where the ants can't get at it. Drop one crumb on the floor and thirty seconds later, hundreds of the little beasts will be all over it."

* * *

As opposed to the previous year, in 2009 my progress grinds to a complete halt. I still haven't gotten to the bottom of the emotional issues that underlie my health problem and as a result, my skin condition has stopped improving.

The ceremonial house is at capacity. Thirty guests are preparing themselves for a journey into the unknown. I'm tired of the status quo and decide to force the issue. On my insistence, Alberto pours me almost a full cup of ayahuasca—double what I would normally consider a sensible amount. Hamilton glances over at its contents and feigns astonishment. "*Está bravo, maestro,*" he says to Alberto, who's blowing tobacco smoke into my cup.

The guests watch me with wide eyes as I down the contents. *Bring it,* I think, as the lilting icaros and trance-inducing rattle of the shacapas carry me into the medicine world.

Within minutes, my sense of peace shatters. I zoom down and down at breakneck speed until I find myself trapped in a multi-coloured maze. I have arrived at the very bowels of hell. I will never, ever escape, even after the effects of the ayahuasca have worn off. From here on, my daily life is going to consist of unrelenting horror.

"I cannot live!" I scream at Hamilton. "I cannot go on any longer. I'm going to kill myself!"

"No you won't," he tells me calmly. "Whether you live or die is not your choice. You have no say in the matter."

And with that, the panic increases. I'm in a pit of darkness, the sides crumbling in, suffocating me. I have no chance of redemption.

"I have the worst life in the entire world!" I bellow. "This is all your fucking fault Hamilton. YOU FUCKING CUNT!"

"That's enough bullshit," he shouts back.

In a flash, he's out of his seat and dragging me to the shower. "This ends now," he says as he pins me in a bear hug from behind.

The water cascades onto both of us. The spray feels like daggers penetrating my flesh. I fight with all my strength to get away. But Hamilton is an indefatigable giant compared to me. I kick. I scream. I will not surrender.

"Say YES to your life!" Hamilton shouts over the noise of the water.

"No. Never. I will never accept this. I never, ever want to live."

"Say YES to your life!" Mimi shouts.

"No. Fuck you."

"Say YES to your life!" shouts Chris.

"Say YES to your life!" shout several voices from the ceremonial house.

But I can't do it. Not even close.

"Pull your shit together now!" Hamilton screams at me. "You've been here long enough. It's time you grew up and took responsibility for your life."

As the water gradually brings the mareación down, my anger begins to subside. Hamilton releases his iron grip. I curl up in a soggy ball on the floor and will myself to disappear. I'm prone only a few minutes before I'm compelled to crawl to the toilet. For the first time in over a year I vomit. Within moments, I'm more at ease and have the energy to change into a dry set of clothes. I force myself to look them in the eyes as I apologise to Hamilton and Mimi.

"It's okay," Mimi reassures me, "it was just those dark spirits that you wouldn't let go of. They make you scared to live, scared to be."

"I know. I just didn't realise what was going on at the time. I couldn't see that it was them speaking, not me—that if I'd just said 'yes' and surrendered, I would've been free."

* * *

Three months later, Chris is convinced that ayahuasca is no longer the answer. I'm at a loss as to what to do.

"You think you're trapped here, that you're in prison. But the door is open. You just have to walk through it," he says.

There's no doubt he's sincere. But I'm still waiting for the ever-elusive breakthrough. In addition to releasing the emotional pain of my illness, I need to let go of all the sadness and loneliness of the past. I can't leave until this is done. How desperately I want to cry but I cannot. Even now, after more than two hundred ceremonies, the torment remains locked inside.

Back in Iquitos, our conversation plays in my head, as though on a loop. Someone or something is trying to tell me that Chris is right. I stubbornly refuse to listen. I've committed to staying here until I'm healed, no matter what.

To my surprise, with each passing day I become more aware of a shift occurring within my psyche. Finally, like an avalanche initiated by the weight of a single snowflake something gives, and I realise that Chris is right. Without any conscious decision on my part, I am done with ayahuasca. I've gone as far as I can go here. It is time for me to move on. That's why the emotional purge didn't happen in ceremony, why I couldn't say, "yes" to my life.

"Your healing isn't going to happen the way you think it will," Hamilton told me a few weeks back. I look within and realise that I was turning to Hamilton and the ayahuasca to heal me. That's why I got stuck. Ayahuasca is not a magic cure for all ailments. It supports and helps transformation—only when one is ready to change. It helped me arrive at this place of recognition and acceptance. Now, the next step is to leave here and live. Chris was right. I'm not trapped.

My God, the change I've been waiting for has just happened. I laugh to myself. I laugh *at* myself. When I tell Hamilton I'm leaving he nods knowingly and says, "When the medicine finally moves, it moves quickly."

I need to stop trying to "heal" myself and start living, face my fears. I must stop focusing on healing because by doing so I'm unconsciously reinforcing the fact that I'm still sick, hence feeding the illness. Moving forward will remove the energetic blockage. I've been connected to the idea of *wanting* to be healthy, and so I've experienced just that—*wanting* to be healthy. Instead, what I must do is recognise that I am healed and whole *now*. To have what I want, I have to give up the idea that it's lacking at all.

"It's totally illogical, but makes perfect sense. It's so much harder this way though," I half-jokingly complain.

"No. It's neither easier nor harder. It is *living*. And you'll find it's much better than worrying about or fearing life," Hamilton says. "To live you simply have to live, to actively participate in life."

So I'd been thinking life, rather than living it. Now I understand. I feel it in my heart.

The next day, I tell Chris the good news.

"It's the right decision," he nods, a wide grin reaching for his ears. "This is a tremendous time of growth for you—the start of a new life. Now that you're ready, change can happen quickly. You can help a lot of people after what you've been through. Remember, we teach best what we most need to learn."

Chris is a very private person, which is why I cherish the closeness that has grown between us. I have so much respect for him and the work he does.

That night, I dream of a flame flickering so feebly, the slightest breeze threatens to snuff it out. I awake knowing I must seek out experiences and relationships that inspire me so my flame will burn more brightly. In this way my body will get the message that there is a reason not only to survive but to thrive.

Now I understand that the gift of the eczema is the opportunity to transcend life circumstance, to know the radiance that exists within me and expresses itself through me when I'm grounded in truth and love.

*　*　*

After being a prisoner in this ramshackle city for more than two years, I've found my way out. I pick up my bag and close the door to my flat, never turning back.

CHAPTER 12
A Different Approach to Life

I cannot do this. I cannot live this life. I have no choice but to kill myself. These thoughts return louder than ever, taunting me, goading me anew into believing there is no hope.

I tried and I failed. Time to give up.

Within weeks of arriving home, my skin condition has worsened yet again. I was convinced leaving Peru was the right decision. I was so certain that my life was moving forwards. Now I'm back to square one. Housebound once more, I'm stifled by depression.

I put my head in my hands and sob as I sit slumped next to my parents at the kitchen table. My mom holds me tenderly, tears trailing down her face.

"Look at these boots I've just bought from the market. They're different sizes, aren't I stupid?" she says with a forced laugh.

I feel like I'm dying inside. *How can she bear my being like this?*

Once my tears abate, words come tumbling unchecked from my mouth. I tell my parents what ayahuasca really is. I tell them about my spiritual awakening and my new-found belief in God. I tell them that I used to take drugs. I tell them about the African witchcraft incident. I tell them how close I came to committing suicide. I let go of everything I'd held onto out of fear, which is as shocking to me as my parents' reaction. Rather than scream at me for being so crazy or disown me, they love and support me unconditionally.

My mom holds me closer and reassures me, "None of that matters now, Mark. It's all in the past. All we need to focus on is getting you better."

"Don't feel guilty. Let that go. Move on," my dad adds.

I spent so long worrying about telling them my secrets because I feared ruining our relationship. Instead, our bond has grown even stronger. To my delight and great relief, I discover that the more I open my heart and trust, the more my fear dissipates.

***

As much as I don't want to go back on the immunosuppressants, it's the only way I can get out and enjoy life. That way I can find out if a more positive attitude will have an impact on my healing. Within a week, the medication is having an effect, which helps lift the depression. Thanks to all the purging in Peru, my skin is better than when I took the tablets last time around, and I can cope without the steroid cream.

The fact that Dr. Basu tells me that I cannot be on the ciclosporin for more than six months makes me even more committed to living every moment to its fullest—to face my fears, take responsibility for my life and open my heart so it can be filled with love.

"Well, it's a marvellous night for a moondance," sings my mobile phone. It's an old friend calling to catch up. She tells me how in love she is with her boyfriend whom she met online and recommends that I give it a go. I've got nothing to lose. Going on a few dates may even help my self-esteem and confidence.

That evening, I check out the eHarmony dating site, attracted by the bold claims about its sophisticated compatibility system, developed from years of intensive research on long-term relationships. After a good forty-five minutes answering their comprehensive questionnaire, I complete the final page and eagerly await my matches.

Instead of a vista of alluring ladies however, all I see is a line of text: "Sorry, you're such a loser that we don't have a single suitable woman for you on our entire site." That might not have been the exact wording of their rejection message, but it was certainly the implication. I'm not sure whether to laugh or curse. So I do both. Nonetheless, I persevere. This time, I'm accepted by Guardian

Soulmates. And to my surprise, later that same day, I receive a message from a lady called Rosie who lives close by.

She has recently returned from a holiday in Peru and wants to know more about me. My mind tells me my skin condition is so bad that I shouldn't respond. While not that noticeable on my face, the eczema is still all over my arms, legs and back.

Yet at the same time, I know that this fear of an intimate relationship was a critical factor in the onset of the illness. Unless I do something, I will never regain my health. I feel trapped. That is, until I remember my recent revelation about how the world really works: the spiritual life is about taking risks—trusting God, leaping and having faith that the net will appear, even when I've absolutely no idea how that could possibly be. I've read about this so many times. It certainly makes a great story. But now I actually have to live it. Shit!

It's time for a totally different way of living—by the seat of my pants, in the moment rather than the future, not knowing what's coming. I must act as if I'm healthy, confident and happy until I feel it in the core of my being. So I send a reply before I can talk myself out of it.

* * *

Two weeks later, I'm on my way to meet Rosie in Bridgnorth. The temperature hasn't risen above freezing for over a week. A thick blanket of snow covers the gently rolling hills, making the picturesque drive to the ancient town even more delightful—quite a contrast from Rosie's hometown of Wolverhampton that I've just passed through. It was recently voted the fifth-worst place to live in the world by Lonely Planet. I decide not to mention this.

"Shropshire's First Fair Trade Town" announces the sign as I approach my destination. Rosie is already there. As I cross the grubby tarmac of the car park, she gets out of her car. I'm struck by her curly red hair. She's petite and looks younger than her twenty-eight years. Or maybe I'm older than I realise and that's how young all twenty-eight-year-olds look. The sight of a pair of shocking pink Wellies on her feet brings a smile to my lips.

As we cross the bridge into town, the icy waters of the River Severn roar beneath us at a pace as though late for meeting with the sea. In summer, the town is a popular tourist destination. On this bitterly cold day, the narrow streets are deserted. We take the 19th century cliff railway up to the High Town, on which, according to the poet Sir John Betjeman, "You feel you are being lifted up to heaven." Personally, I'm just relieved not to have to walk up the two-hundred-plus steps.

With the cafe practically to ourselves, Rosie selects a table by the window. From this height, we have a majestic, panoramic view of the pristine, snow-covered countryside below.

Given this is my first proper date since the ill-fated trip to the ABC Cinema in Walsall some twenty years ago, I spent hours trying to plan conversation topics. I gave up in the end, knowing full well that I would have to explain why I spent so much time in Peru and that it would either be a conversation-stopper because she'd think I was totally nuts or she'd be intrigued and we would have plenty to talk about. The fact that she just returned from a holiday to the Sacred Valley outside of Cusco gives me hope that it will be the latter.

The inevitable question soon comes. With a moment's hesitation, I launch into my story. As I discuss my illness and ayahuasca, Rosie remains expressionless. But I get the feeling she doesn't think I'm a complete freak. And that will do for starters.

I shift the focus to her. She glows as she tells me about her job. She works with children who, because of their special needs, aren't in mainstream education. She co-ordinates the schooling of foster children and teaches those who aren't currently in school. On top of that, she also started her own charity that runs holidays and after-school clubs for the same kids.

Self-assured without being arrogant or aloof, Rosie grew up with a spiritual view of the world thanks to her mother's hippie influence.

"About two years ago, something happened that changed my life completely," she says, lowering her voice. "I don't tell many people about this," she continues with a flicker of a smile.

My heart beats a little faster.

"I was driving down to London, singing loudly, as I often do in the car. I was in a state of total surrender, fully accepting of everything in my life. Suddenly, I started floating out of my body, and I became aware of the perfection of the Universe—that it always was perfect and always will be. I was no longer myself. I was the road, the cars, the trees, the sky, the clouds—everything, all at once. It was more real than any experience I've ever had. Since that day, whenever I'm having a hard time, I remember that feeling and the difficulty vanishes. Whatever's going on in my life is nothing in comparison to the wonder and perfection of that moment."

The afternoon flies by as we discuss life, spirituality, the workings of the Universe and the nature of fear. I talk mostly, maybe a little too much, about my struggles. After all, they've shaped who I am. I frame them positively, ignoring the negative voices that whisper incessantly that I shouldn't be sharing all this.

We eventually become aware of the owner's impatience to close the cafe and head back to the car park. As we say our goodbyes my stomach clenches.

"I've had a great time today, and I'd love to see you again," I tell her, my ears prickling hot.

"Me too, that would be nice," she replies.

"I'll email you," I say and give her a peck on the cheek.

I drive home singing loudly with a smile so wide it hurts my cheeks.

* * *

For once, the endless mental chatter subsides. In this relaxed and open state I feel connected to life, to everything in my bedroom and beyond. Expanding into the space around me, I lose all sense of my self. From this perspective, I'm detached from all the worries and anxieties that have defined me. They lose their significance, their power.

I perceive something else present, and it's trying to flow through me. Instinctively, I know that this sensation is love, my true nature. This love is welling up inside, about to burst forth, but I'm not yet ready to feel it fully.

I tell Rosie all of this, wary of sounding too full of myself—especially as I know she loathes arrogance. I'm too excited and trust that she will recognise the truth behind my words. As I speak, she plays with her hair, then suddenly stops and leans towards me. I'm as naive as they come where body language and flirting is concerned, yet something tells me this is a good sign.

It's astonishingly easy to talk openly with Rosie. We seem to be tuned in to the same frequency. All week I can't stop thinking about her. However, before we take things further, I will have to do what I dread most—be honest about my past. I'm convinced she will think less of me, that I won't be a man in her eyes because of my inability to be in a relationship. Which may well make her decide I'm not the one for her. Regardless, I can feel the medicine spirits inside pushing me to tell her everything.

I must have faith that the Universe has brought me the perfect person to help me along the next stage of my journey. Only once I let go, can I release the fear and fully be myself. If I continue to worry about what she may think, I'll never open up. I decide to view this as an opportunity to trust.

* * *

Rosie invites me over for dinner. She greets me, looking lovelier than ever in an emerald-green dress that sets off the fiery highlights in her hair. After a candlelit meal, we settle on her sofa to watch a documentary about ayahuasca that I took part in whilst in Peru.

"I want to tell you some more about me and my life," I blurt out, immediately sensing her trepidation. *What the hell, too late now.* "As I've mentioned, I'm on a mission of facing and overcoming my fears. My biggest fear is being in an intimate relationship. It's also what I want more than anything.

"When I returned to England I said to the Universe that I was ready for a genuine, loving relationship. I said, 'Bring me the girl who can help me trust in life, trust in God, trust in love. Bring me the girl who I can open up to and who will understand and help me transcend this fear.' And then you showed up."

Twisting her hair around her fingers, Rosie smiles at me in a way I can't quite identify. I imagine excusing myself with a curt, "Sorry, I've gotta go." Yet I press on, "No doubt I'll get better because I understand how I got sick. This might sound strange, but it happened because I didn't love myself. Since I felt unlovable I was consumed by fear and loneliness."

I search her face for some sign of approval or encouragement. Nothing. I look down at my hands trembling in my lap and continue, "Okay, the truth is I'm scared to open my heart. I'm scared of you judging me. But I'm actually willing to take the risk because I'm starting to believe all of this is my own crap and that maybe you won't think I'm pathetic. My self-confidence is growing all the time. But, um, obviously, I've got some work to do. Which I can't do alone."

I jerk my gaze up from my hands to meet her eyes and glimpse a glimmer of approval, which emboldens me to continue. I'm shocked by my courage to say what comes next.

"I want to share my life with you. And I want to share yours. If you're willing to join me, I think we're in for one seriously amazing adventure. It'll require patience, kindness and understanding on your part, so that I feel safe to let this stuff go. The more I learn to trust and let go, the healthier I should become physically and mentally."

Now stone-faced, Rosie blinks a couple of times, her mouth falls open and quickly snaps shut. She doesn't utter a word for an agonising thirty seconds. Regardless, I feel lighter, freer. Peace envelops me.

"I'm a very happy person, and I love my life," she says eventually. "But I also have a fear of intimacy, and I haven't been in a long-term relationship either."

Now it's my turn to look shell-shocked. A tear escapes from the corner of Rosie's eye.

"That's my deepest fear and biggest wish too," she says. "The most important lesson my soul has to learn in this lifetime is to find the trust to be in an intimate relationship. I'd like to do that with you."

I take her in my arms and feel the warmth of her body against mine. We melt into each other.

SHEDDING THE LAYERS

* * *

Even though Rosie tells me that my skin condition doesn't bother her in the slightest, only part of me believes her. The other part doesn't want to. Her acceptance brings up resistance as strong as my most negative core belief—that I'm unlovable. As exposed as I feel sharing my fears with her, allowing myself to be vulnerable is the next step.

My mind must be healed, not my skin. I'm so tired of the mental conflict. I'm ready to dive into this relationship and experience all that it has to offer. I'm willing to accept any hurt that it may bring because at least that way, I am feeling. I am living.

Sharing my truth with Rosie inspires me to confront another fear—public speaking. I figure speaking from my heart in front of complete strangers should do wonders for my confidence and may help me heal.

I join Toastmasters, a worldwide organisation designed to improve public speaking and communication skills. As much as the idea of giving a speech to a room full of people terrifies me, it's as though the decision has already been made for me.

After going to one meeting as a guest, I become a member and request to give my first speech as soon as possible. I immediately know its theme. It's the story of the last five years condensed into five minutes, minus any reference to ayahuasca, shamanism and spirits. Best to save that for later.

I practise ten times a day over the next two weeks. I even record myself. As painful as it is to listen to my own voice, it's an excellent tool for improvement. I also spend time visualising myself in the room, feeling relaxed and having fun while I hold the audience in rapt attention. My body tingles at the thought of delivering the speech live.At the next Toastmasters gathering, I arrive early. My cheeks burn, and beads of sweat fringe my hairline as I scan the room. Soon I'll have to stand up and share some very personal information with two-dozen strangers. The room closes in on me. I wish I could bolt for the door, but a heavy weight holds my muscles firmly in place. When the evening officially commences I cannot keep my hands from shaking.

A succession of people take their turn at speaking. I can't hear a word they're saying. I'm focused on taking long, slow breaths and relaxing my body. I tune back in to what's going on around me just in time to hear the club's president introduce me:

"With his first speech at Toastmasters, entitled "The Gift of Fear", please give an extra-warm welcome to Mark."

I walk to the front in a daze. I've memorised my speech so thoroughly that the words blessedly begin to come out of their own accord. After a few seconds, my tension dissipates, just a little. I do my best to make eye contact with the audience. As I look at the sea of faces staring impassively back at me, the mental chatter becomes vociferous:

Look at them. They're not interested in what I'm saying. They're bored senseless. Who do I think I am to be standing up here telling people about my life? They think I'm arrogant. They can see how scared I am.

On and on it goes, forcing me to focus even more intently on delivering the speech. It comes out slowly, clearly and with a reasonable degree of passion and feeling. Before I know it, I'm walking back to my seat to the sound of rapturous applause, peeling my T-shirt away from my back as I go.

At Toastmasters everybody provides brief written feedback to each speaker. Although the ethos of the club is to always be supportive and not criticise, I'm still blown away by the level of praise. One paper reads, "The best speech I have ever heard at Toastmasters," another, "A competition-winning speech." Even though it's always easier for me to focus on what I didn't do perfectly, I look past the imperfections and am elated with my first effort, especially when I win the Best Speaker of the Evening award.

I walk out of the building feeling eight feet tall, eagerly planning my next speech.

* * *

We walk hand-in-hand around the garden of her sister's flat in London. Leaves tipped with dew glint in the morning sunlight. I inhale the familiar aroma of freshly mowed grass. Light-headed and beaming with joy, I'm captivated by Rosie's eyes, hazel, the pupils ringed with flares of gold.

"You should have heard the applause," I tell her as excitedly as a boy scoring the winning goal in a cup final. "I was so nervous at first but then, the words just magically started tumbling out. I felt like a superstar." *Oh no, now she'll think I'm arrogant bastard. Why'd I have to say that?*

"That's because you are a superstar," she whispers into my ear as she threads her fingers through mine. "I'm so pleased. Well done you," she continues, grasping my hand more tightly.

My heart soars. Then, Rosie unclasps her hand, leaving mine abandoned. The weight of loneliness drops into the pit of my stomach yet lifts as quickly as it sank when I realise she removed her hand only to give my arm a squeeze. I grin like an idiot. I've never felt this close to someone, let alone a woman.

I dutifully accompany her as she tucks a chocolate with a note wrapped around it inside a small crevice in an oak tree. Creating a treasure hunt for her mom's birthday, she continues to the next hiding spot.

Before I know it, the sun has risen high in the sky. I check my watch and wince as I see that it's 12:30, time for Rosie to meet her mom. I wish I could stay longer, but I certainly don't want to crowd her, as she likes time to do her own thing. Anyway, we'll see each other this evening for her mom's celebration.

In his crisp, white shirt and silken black tie, the Indian waiter laughs as he pours me yet another blessed glass of water. I look up at him with a mixture of awe and greed. The sweat that fringed my forehead at the first bite of Chicken Korma is now trickling down my beet-red face into the collar of my shirt. I'd sooner be facing my demons in the ceremonial house than be sitting in this curry house. But Rosie's family loves Indian food, and I want to make a good impression.

"Welcome to the family," Rosie's sister says, playfully kicking me in the shins.

I nod and smile politely, furtively wiping my nose. "Th-thanks," I splutter.

Rosie's mom notices me struggling and says, waving a piece of naan, "This is for Mark. The dear can't handle spice apparently." I gratefully accept her offering.

"Why didn't you order something less spicy?" Rosie asks, squeezing my thigh under the table.

"I ordered the mildest dish on the menu," I reply, reaching for the water jug.

Rosie leans in more closely, I lean away not wanting her to get such a close look at the sweat streaming down my face, "I know you said you couldn't tolerate chillies very well, but I had no idea it was this bad!"

"I'm just a sensitive guy, I guess," I say, with a cheeky grin.

"You poor thing, I'll take good care of you," she replies, patting my leg.

* * *

If only we could spend more time like this. However, Rosie cannot see me nearly as much as I would like. She simply has more going on in her life than I do. She says she also needs time alone to decompress and feels pressured to be with me whenever she does have a spare moment.

When we're together I'm content and comfortable. Unfortunately, as much as I love being with her, I'm growing more and more dissatisfied. We spend only a few hours a week together. I constantly fret about whether the situation will ever change. But I've waited such a long time for a relationship that I'm willing to compromise.

Nonetheless, I admire Rosie's willingness to face issues in order to learn and grow from them. After I tell her about my concerns, she admits that she keeps herself so busy because she's scared to allow me more into her life. A troubled childhood put her through a long and painful process of self-discovery. Having fought hard to find peace and independence, she's scared that if we get too close, she will lose herself and everything she has worked so hard to achieve.

This is tough for her and I do my very best to remain patient. At the same time, I have to look after myself, too. I tell her in a kind, direct way that if she's serious about being in a relationship, she will have to find more time for me. I want to be with her. But she has to want it too. She has to decide where her priorities lie.

* * *

After much consideration, Rosie reorganises her schedule so we can be together more often. As the weeks turn to months, we become more intimate. Ironically, now that we see each other regularly she has become reluctant to show me affection. Consequently, I end up pestering her for attention, which only pushes her farther away.

She's making an effort, but I'm frustrated. As much as I try not to let my irritation show she picks up on it.

"You have to give me space," she declares. "Over the past couple of weeks I've felt like my head is going to explode."

Now I'm no expert, but an exploding head doesn't seem like the ideal basis for a relationship.

"Whatever I give you, it's not enough. It never will be enough," she hisses in exasperation. "I've got no idea what you want. But whatever it is, I can't give it to you. I'm fine on my own. You add to my life, and I love being with you, but I don't need anything from you to be fulfilled. I want you to see me as a bonus to everything else in your life, not as a solution to your problems. If we split up, I'd be sad, but I'd cope. You're looking for me to make you happy, and I can't do that. You have to find it inside yourself."

Her words knock the wind out of me. We're in a busy pub on a Sunday evening, and I can't prevent myself from crying.

* * *

The very next day, the plant spirits tell me it's time to go back to Peru—for three weeks, not three years. Apparently it's time for new lessons and further assistance from the ayahuasca.

The bright blue sky and warm sun heralds the end of winter and the beginning of a new cycle of growth and rebirth. The quality of the light is sensational, and as I drive past a majestic oak tree, I burst out laughing. I cannot help it. It is delightful.

This is the perfect time to tell my parents of my decision: My mom bursts into tears because I'll be away for her birthday. My dad tells me he's disappointed and calls me selfish. He thinks that I'm wasting my time; that I spent years in the jungle with no effect. I explain all the changes I went through. I try to explain that I'm getting better all the time and that the physical illness is tied to my fears and my healing, to spiritual awakening.

Unfortunately, there's nothing I can say that will make my dad comprehend what I feel and know. As frustrating as it may be, I come to accept that he's on his own path, and this is an important test of my integrity. I'm being asked to be authentic. I know my truth, and I must live it. I'm being asked to grow up, to be an adult in my parents' presence. I resist the strong temptation to revert to an angry teenager.

Later, my dad comes and knocks on my door. He tells me that he will support any decision I make and doesn't want to fall out over this. He hugs me for the first time I can remember. My face quickly becomes soaked with tears.

CHAPTER 13
Epiphany

I look out the window at the pristine snow-capped peaks of the Andes that give way to the familiar Amazonian expanse of green trees and brown rivers. Soon we'll be landing in Iquitos which will be a different city to me this time around.

I change all the routines I created before to banish the memories of previous stays. I stay in a new hostel. I have a new room at camp. I sit on the opposite side of the ceremonial house, and I swap the plastic, straight-backed chair for a rocking chair. I also make sure that I spend more time socialising, rather than lying on my bed, fretting about the upcoming ceremony. Now I know how detrimental thinking can be to the whole ayahuasca process. Once in ceremony, the mind is of zero value. Thinking is not just pointless, it's counterproductive.

Rather than focus on healing my body or pushing away any uncomfortable feelings that may arise, I resolve to observe without attaching to them. Hopefully, the physical healing will happen naturally as these emotions are released.

This night, when the kerosene lamps are extinguished we're not left in complete darkness. The full moon's hazy glow, outlines the group. But one of us is not present—for the first time in eight years Hamilton has missed a ceremony. Even when he had dengue fever and was unable to stand up, he still managed to hold ceremonies, wheeling himself around the room in his over-sized office chair to give venteadas. On this occasion he had no choice. A motocross accident left him with a dislocated and fractured hip.

"I went off a sixty-foot jump on my new bike for the first time," he said when I visited him in hospital a few days ago. "The jump was awesome. The landing, not so good."

"Was that your biggest accident yet?" I asked him, knowing he'd had several others.

"Dude, being born was my biggest accident!"

The doctors in Iquitos told him that he needed an operation. He wanted a second opinion and sent a copy of his X-ray to the US. In the meantime, he discharged himself from hospital and came out to camp, spending yesterday lying on a stack of mattresses in the ceremonial house with two bags of rice hanging off his ankle as traction. Today, he left for Lima immediately after having gotten word from the doctors in the States that an operation was vital.

As the rhythmic sounds of the shacapas signal the commencement of the ceremony, I remind myself of my task for tonight—focus on my heart. Every time a thought enters my head, I let it go and return my awareness to the area around my chest. Initially, my concentration extends to about two seconds. Ayahuasca is superb at bringing unconscious or barely conscious aspects of myself into stark awareness. Tonight I become cognisant of how short my attention span and focus are.

When I'm not quick enough to recognise that my mind has latched onto a thought, it immediately leads to another and another and another. Before I know it, I'm completely lost, once again believing all the crazy stories that my mind concocts. I feel the familiar sensation of fear as darkness creeps up from all sides and begins to smother me.

Rather than panic and descend farther into the gloom, I stop. There's no need to engage with these thoughts and feelings. They have no power over me, cannot do anything to me. I take a deep breath and relax into the experience, relax into the medicine. Over two hundred ceremonies later I finally discover genuine trust. I know beyond doubt that I am safe, and I calmly surrender completely.

The darkness vanishes, leaving me in a state of stillness and receptivity. Without any effort, I am in my heart. I am consciously connected to it, a sensation that is utterly foreign to me. All this time I was looking for my heart—a sense of love and connectedness—without success. Now, the moment I give up searching I find it. And where is it? Exactly where Hamilton was telling me for years—right where I am. The idea of opening the heart is actually a misnomer. The heart is always open. It's just a matter of whether I'm emotionally connected to it or stuck in my head.

I am present in the moment, not lost in thought. Finally, I experience love—real, profound love. Joy and serenity wash up and down my body in waves, from toes to head and back again. I finally understand all I've heard Hamilton say over the last seven years and all I've read in spiritual books over the last fifteen years.

I see the entire Universe; it is right here, inside my heart. It is perfect. I am perfect. The answer to every question I've had and ever will have is in my heart, always. My heart knows what to do in any situation. This is not some romantic, idealistic view of life. It is absolutely real and true. That I don't know what to do in any given scenario is nothing more than a story my mind has been creating—a story I used to believe.

The work is not to face and overcome the negativity, my fears and the past. That is actively doing—a force of will, a construct of the mind. There really is nothing to face, nothing to change, except my perception. All the pain and suffering that was trapped inside me, that I was scared to confront, doesn't exist, except as thoughts. The moment I choose to be present and witness my thoughts, all conflict ceases. The mental chatter subsides, leaving a direct experience of life. Now that I've broken through my resistance into a new way of living—in my heart—the "work" is simply to stay right here.

"Just look for love and you will see it everywhere," the spirits tell me. "In a flower, in a smile, in music, in food. The whole world is made of pure love. Look for it, and when you follow it, you will go deeper and deeper into the experience of love. Just relax, surrender and allow it to guide you."

By remaining present, by bathing in the blissful state of *being*, all that exists is love, and love unifies everything. There's no need to fix anything because nothing is, or ever was, wrong. I just have to *remember* love.

"Ultimately, it is love that heals," my acupuncturist Laurence told me all those years ago. Back then, those words meant nothing to me. Now I understand but in a different way. Love has shown me that there is nothing to heal, that I am, and always have been, perfect. Love removes all discord, making life effortless. And as long as I don't get in the way, it will flow through me in a never-ending stream of beauty. These revelations are so obvious and elemental that I explode with laughter. I sound uncannily like a donkey, "Hee haw, hee haw."

Life is an infinite party... and God is the DJ.

"I GET IT! I GET IT!" I shout.

I had to search all over the world first and not find happiness, peace or love. It's only in this moment of total surrender, of no effort, that I experience these miraculous emotions. As soon as I stopped looking, believing they were lacking, I became receptive. And in doing so I discovered that I have always been whole.

I see life for what it really is—eternal. I am eternal. Time is a creation of the mind. When thinking stops, time disappears and eternity is revealed. Knowing that I was never born and can never die my fear of death disappears. In its place is the certainty that what we call death is the best thing that can ever happen in life. The freedom of the present moment must be a blip compared to the moment when a lifetime of burdens is lifted.

Another point that Hamilton made earlier rings true, "Our perception and understanding of time must shift. Everybody experiences life through the veil of their own personal philosophy—no more than a mishmash of thoughts. It's all just a story. When you look with your eyes, you see the story. When you look with your heart, you see the truth."

Now I see there is no past, nor future. Whenever I've thought of the past or the future, it has become my present experience. The truth is, all that exists is this very moment—a realisation that frees me from everything I believed was my past and feared would be my future. Since all problems are constructs of the mind, they can never be resolved intellectually. Instead, one needs to shift consciousness to see that there is nothing wrong.

As Hamilton has said, "The healing modality is focused on the person. We need to move beyond it, into the mystical. Nothing in manifestation can fix anything else in manifestation. Thoughts do not create or manifest anything. Thoughts are the expression of creation and are manifest. Love ends the narrative. And when the story ends, there is liberation."

"Do not try to live life, let life live you," I hear the spirits say.

All this time I've been trying to get somewhere, trying to heal, when my disease and supposed lack of progress were nothing more than an illusion, a trick of the mind. There is nothing to achieve, nothing to do, nowhere to go. There is only being. As humans we are already enlightened, and we know this only when we are connected to our hearts. The instant I remember my heart, there is no state of dis-ease or lacking.

Furthermore, the whole notion of struggle is just a story—albeit a very compelling one. I had to stop striving to live from the heart in order to know I always was. I merely *thought* I wasn't. Loving is actually the only thing any of us innately knows how to do. I was scared of loving, of connecting to my heart, because I thought it would be too overwhelming. Like maybe my head would explode. The reality is quite the opposite. It is gentle, kind and, well, loving! It's the most natural sensation in the world.

Divine Love and Oneness is who I really am—I heard and read this hundreds of times and understood the concept intellectually. I could believe it. But belief counts for nothing. Belief is based in the mind. The mind believes. The heart knows. Beyond any rational argument, beyond any logical explanation, I no longer believe; I *know*. Hamilton's spirit is with me, watching my transformation with delight.

"Ah, welcome," he says. "You have freed your mind. I'm proud of you."

* * *

The next day my body is glowing inside and out. I feel completely alert and relaxed. The flowers and trees shimmer with breathtaking splendour. My footsteps on the path are so light I might be floating across camp. I sit on a step and watch the iridescent wings of a blue morpho butterfly glide past. To my left, the tiny figure of a hummingbird darts into vision, hovers over a brilliant yellow flower and is gone in the blink of an eye.

Inside the main house, Chris is preparing to give a talk on astrology. My knowledge of the subject consists of flicking through one of his books in the camp library and having him study my chart a couple of years ago. The accuracy of his reading was amazing. He knew so much about me—the way I think and act, how I view the world, and the issues I've had to deal with in my life—without us ever having spoken about them.

As he speaks now, I'm don't want him to stop. I'm like an inquisitive child wanting to know everything. After an hour-long overview and answering many of my questions, he gives me the titles of a number of books to read as an introduction to the subject—a subtle hint that he's explained enough for now.

At the first opportunity back in town, I head straight for the internet cafe where I order all of the books and spend hours devouring a mass of astrological information. Meanwhile, I allow the medicine's deluge of revelations to sink in slowly. I don't think about them or what it all means. I just enjoy this serene state of presence.

Now, I'm able to explore Iquitos in a way that I couldn't in my years of living here. I feel like a tourist. I feel like a human being. I feel pretty damn good. In Belen Market, I meet a young man who offers to give me a tour of Lower Belen, the poorest district in the poorest region of Peru. Home to 15,000 people who cannot afford a plot of land on which to build, they live on the Itaya River, a tributary of the Amazon. Their rickety floating houses are built on balsa wood rafts, all tied to each other to ensure they don't float away in the strong currents.

I step gingerly into the wobbling canoe and sit as close to the centre of the wooden bench as possible to avoid being splashed by the rancid water. Houses in Lower Belen have neither bathrooms nor running water. One man's toilet is another man's bathing water.

There's a whole other world down here—floating bars and restaurants, as well as churches and schools built on stilts. Children wave excitedly as we cruise slowly down their main street. Some show off their acrobatic skills by performing somersaults and back flips from their porches into the water, while others are hard at work scrubbing the family's clothes. In the most unlikely places all over Latin America you'll find football pitches, and Belen is no exception.

Although at this time of year, only the top twelve inches of the goalposts are visible.

Government officials have described this place as "The Horror of Peru" due to the low quality of education, sanitation and healthcare. Yet it has a real charm. It's cooler and more peaceful than the city. At sunset, the locals' description of it as "The Venice of the Amazon" seems less of a joke than before. But then again, I'm visiting for an hour and don't have to experience the harsh reality of life down here.

I hold my breath as I get out of the boat, the stench strong enough to make me wretch. I go to buy avocados from a street vendor. Having remembered me, he strikes up a conversation, wanting to know what I was doing in Iquitos when I lived here. I tell him about my skin condition and the treatment with ayahuasca. He then speaks passionately about his own bad health. What the doctors gave him did no good, so he turned to a local healer who prescribed a mixture of plants from the jungle. They made him vomit, but within just a few days, all of his symptoms were gone. As he's telling me this, a man comes to buy avocados, but the vendor ignores him.

I'd bought produce from this guy dozens of times in the past, but this is the first conversation we've had. All over town, I converse with the locals, relishing the feel of their beautiful language on my tongue. In the past, I was reluctant to engage with them, assuming they just wanted money. Now, in this tranquil state, it's clear that these people want nothing more than to offer their friendliness and wish me a pleasant stay in their city. Everywhere I go, people recognise me: hotel staff, waiters and waitresses, even moto-taxi drivers and random people in the street. I have no idea who many of them are, but they know my name. I feel like a movie star.

Later, I meet Mimi for a drink at a cafe overlooking the Plaza de

SHEDDING THE LAYERS

Armas. Objectively, Iquitos is the same place as when I was here a year ago—the same heat, the same noise, the same people. But now, it's a wholly different experience.

"You're experiencing Iquitos as different because you've cleansed your mind of negativity. Ultimately, this affects you both inside *and* outside, making your inner experience, as well as the external world, a positive reality, free from judgment and fear."

* * *

A week later, at the end of ceremony Hamilton says, "Can you hear the insects? That is you. Can you see how in ayahuasca everything is alive? That is you. That is your life force. Do you notice how the sounds of the insects get louder as the ceremony begins? That's because your life force is intensifying. Life is just a perception of the mind. It's not actually happening 'out there'. You are everything. Which means 'out there'," he says extending his arms and pausing for a moment, "and 'in here'," he continues, bringing his hands to his heart, "are one and the same."

Considering the notion that life is simply a perception of the mind, I reflect upon how my relationship with Rosie is nothing more than a way of relating to one other. I was looking to her to provide something that I perceived as missing. Of course she couldn't give me what I wanted. The *wanting* itself was the issue, not the object of my wants. If she were able to give me everything I asked for I still wouldn't be satisfied because my mind would find something else that was lacking. It goes on forever seeking what's wrong, searching for the thing or the person that will solve the "problem". A relationship can't solve anything because no problem exists, except as a thought.

I breathe this truth into every cell of my body. I feared that my time with Rosie would be over since she wasn't giving me what I wanted, but now I realise that the same would be true with anyone. I remember what Rosie brings to my life—kindness, companionship, humour, playfulness, stimulating conversation, intimacy, her acceptance of me, her smile, her laughter and her beauty.

I wasted most of our time together wanting more. In fact, I've spent my entire life wanting more, whether it was money, food, beer, drugs or love. But there is no "more". This moment is everything there is. And I can't have more than everything.

As if reading my mind, Hamilton speaks, "You cannot become more than you already are because you already are everything. You just need to remember that. Remember what you already know. We always want more. We strive to achieve. We compete in the Human Race. We want to win. But what we forget is that we are already at the finish line. We have already won. We are already holding the trophy. The prize is being alive. The prize is being in a body."

* * *

I've never felt so relaxed before a ceremony. I've never been excited to drink ayahuasca. Tonight I really am. Previously, I understood intellectually that my illness stemmed from a lack of love. Now, I feel it. Now, I *know* it. Finally, love is not just an idea; it is an experience that fortifies me.

As the icaros begin, I focus on my breath, inhaling light and love and feeling it penetrate to my core. My life force returns. My fingers and toes vibrate as they awaken from the longest of sleeps. Energy flows through my arms and legs. They twitch and jerk as the toxic energies in my nervous system dissipate. I feel alive. I feel. I don't think, *I feel*. I am right here, completely present in my body, not lost in the outer reaches of my mind. A tingling sensation courses through my limbs, torso, neck and head. Shockingly, I'm actually pleased and grateful to have a body. I stretch and am in heaven.

I catch a glimpse of my hand. It's mesmerising, the funniest-looking thing I've ever seen. It's also unbelievably amazing. I wiggle my fingers and burst out laughing. I wave my hands around and crack up again. I love my hands so much.

I cannot stop laughing. I'm in such ecstasy that I may burst.

"It's good that you finally get the joke, Inglés," Chris says to me. "It's only taken three hundred ceremonies."

"Hey, give me some credit. It's only two hundred and seventy. It was worth the wait, though. It's a good joke."

"I've got a new icaro for you," he says. "Check this out:"

I'm a back seat driver to my life, always crashing into my strife
But if I relax and enjoy the view, I won't skid in all my poo

Da da vroom vroom, beep beep, vroom vroom beep
Vroom vroom, beep beep, vroom vroom vroom

God's the guy driving up in front, he's the dude and I'm the grunt
God's the guy driving up in front, he's the dude and I'm the grunt

Da da vroom vroom, beep beep, vroom vroom beep
Vroom vroom, beep beep, vroom vroom vroom

Life is just a pretty dream, a big bowl of peaches and cream
Life can taste so very sweet, as long as I don't piss on my back seat

*Da da vroom vroom, beep beep, vroom vroom beep
Vroom vroom, beep beep, vroom vroom vroom*

*I´m a back seat driver to my life, always crashing into my strife
But if I relax and enjoy the view, I won't skid in all my poo*

*Sometimes I try to interfere, by taking drugs and drinking beer
Then my mind is full of fear, how I wish it was so clear*

*God's the guy driving up in front, he's the dude and I'm the grunt
God's the guy driving up in front, he's the dude and I'm the grunt*

*Da da vroom vroom, beep beep, vroom vroom beep
Vroom vroom, beep beep, vroom vroom vroom*

*Life is just a pretty dream, a big bowl of strawberries and cream
Oh my my it can taste so sweet, as long as I don't piss on that damn back seat*

Outside the ceremonial house, the stars are out en masse. As I breathe in the sweet night air, the stars rush towards me, filling me with the light of a thousand galaxies. As I exhale, they recede into the night sky. I drift back to my bed, sensing the gentle strength of the giant Renaco tree that stands guard over the centre of the camp.

I fall into a deep sleep and am back in the city at the Max Augustín stadium watching a match of the Iquitos football team, CNI. After a few minutes in the crowd, I suddenly find myself on the pitch, one of the players. I can't stand still and pace back and forth near the corner flag. *How'd I get here? I can't play this game like a pro. If I have to play, people will see me for the fraud I am.*

SHEDDING THE LAYERS

Despite my best efforts to stay inconspicuous, the ball is passed to me. Instinctively, I evade a sliding tackle and slip the ball to a teammate. As I race into the opposing half, the ball is played back into my path. Adrenaline pumping, I advance before unleashing a thunderbolt shot that crashes into the top corner of the net.

* * *

It has been over a week since Hamilton returned from his successful operation in Lima. He must be tired and in severe discomfort, but it doesn't stop him from holding ceremony and giving daily talks. His words expand my recent realisations: "Inside you there is a voice of integrity that expresses complete certainty. This voice speaks only from the experience of being you. It is not a thought. It is the expression of your truth and, if you follow it, will never lead you astray.

"When you live from that voice, everything flows. What flows is not always what we call 'good'. That which *is* simply flows. It's a voice you listen for, by being quiet, receptive, focused. It's up to you alone to figure out how to listen to your voice of integrity. How that looks will be different for everyone. When you are active and thinking, you experience self. When you are receptive, you experience God, divinity, wholeness, love, and you live from your heart centre.

"Experience is complete and whole and perfect in and of itself and cannot happen again. Everything happens only once. No experience in life affects any other. Therefore, without any past there is no notion of trauma and nothing to heal."

Focus is the key. What I focus on is what I experience. I used to think that I had terrible focus, but it's actually impossible not to be focused. In reality, I was focusing on many disparate things in rapid succession. The longer I can hold my focus on love, the more I enjoy life.

* * *

Tomorrow morning I return to England. Finally, I've seen the other side of ayahuasca—the one filled with light, love and divinity—that I watched so many guests experience week after week as I wallowed in misery.

Tonight, the ayahuasca gives me a parting opportunity to learn yet more. As I find that quiet place of receptivity, the understanding that life is unfolding precisely as it's supposed to begins to penetrate deeper and deeper. Life is perfect for the simple reason that it can only ever be what it is; it can only ever be *this*. The all-encompassing whole of everything that is even includes the thought that life could or should be different in some way.

"What makes life interesting is the amplitude of experience," Hamilton tells us. "That includes all the things we call 'good' and 'bad', 'right' and 'wrong'. These are just labels, structures in our psyche. In short, they are nothing more or less than experiences."

Therefore, nothing can ever really be good or bad. It can only ever be what it is. I dislike violence (amongst many other things). But that doesn't make it wrong. Violence is not inherently bad. Violence is violence. It doesn't mean that I should like it or condone it. All I must do is acknowledge it as being the only thing it can possibly be.

A "spiritual" life is not better than any other life. Every life is equally important, equally unique and equally purposeful. Every single person is living the right life for them in that moment. No one can be doing anything other than what they are doing. I go on a journey to go on a journey, not to get anywhere. Spiritual growth can't take me anywhere. There is no destination. When I stop to see where I am, I find myself where I've always been—right here.

I spent so much time thinking life should be different, wishing it were different. My life was made up of regret, blame, guilt, shame, plans, hopes, fears, wants and desires. None of them have any bearing on what will happen. Life is living me, not the other way around. Just like the spirits said, all I have to do is let life flow through me and move in harmony with it.

The knowledge that I'm not the one doing my life is tremendously liberating—all the energy I was exhausting by constantly fleeing from the present moment becomes available to enjoy what is actually happening, right here, right now. And there's no better experience than Now—it's all there is.

Since life is perfect, and made of love, every single moment is perfect and full of love. As long as I remember this, it doesn't matter what's currently happening, as it's an expression of love, and I can come to no harm. No one and no thing can ever really hurt me; I can only *think* that I've been hurt. My true nature is untouchable and unchanging, a perfect manifestation of Divine Love, which gives me the freedom to express exactly who I am in this moment. Since I can be nothing other than who I am at any given time, accepting myself becomes easy.

Contrary to much of the spiritual literature that I've read, I realise that Mark does not create or manifest anything. Who I really am, my true nature, is Creation which manifests the self, i.e. Mark, and everything else. Therefore, everything happens just as is it meant to. Consequently, all of us will achieve exactly what we are here to achieve. We cannot do otherwise. Which means failure is impossible, and we are always on the right path. Even when we *think* we're not, that thought *is* our path! Even when we don't understand anything that's happening, and it feels like our life is completely falling apart, that's precisely how we're supposed to be feeling in that moment. And even in those darkest of moments we are being held, safe and protected by God.

Much of the worrying that I do comes from trying to plan how I want the future to look. Now I know better. Now I know all of these thoughts are irrelevant. They have absolutely no bearing on what will happen. All I can do is continue to be present to whatever is happening right now and enjoy it right now.

I rock gently in my chair as the final ceremony draws to a close. A kerosene lamp is relit and the assistants and shamans receive a well-earned and rapturous round of applause. The atmosphere in the ceremonial house is celebratory as another remarkable week of medicine comes to a close.

"*Todo bom,*" muses Alberto in Portuguese, lighting a mapacho. "It's all good."

"*Muito bom,*" agrees Chris.

"How was your night?" I ask the lady to my left, who is clutching a tissue and looking somewhat bewildered.

"Oh, it was wonderful, except for the moment when I puked out of my nose and got a piece of food stuck in one of my nostrils. I blew it out, and it rebounded off the sink basin, flew up and hit me in the eye!"

Ayahuasca is fabulous medicine, but it is not always glamorous.

"*Gracias por toda su ayuda, maestro*", I say to Alberto, thanking him for his help.

"*De nada. Trabajamos duro hasta la muerte. Entonces descansamos.*" "You're welcome," he says. "We work hard until we die, then we'll rest."

"I look forward to that day." Hamilton says before adding, "*El único problema con la muerte es que todas las mujeres son esqueletos.*"

The sound of Alberto's hearty laughter fills the entire room and sets everyone else off even though most have no idea what Hamilton said. I translate: "The only problem with death is that all the women are skeletons."

I look over at Hamilton kicking back in his leather chair, hands behind his head in a self-satisfied stretch. We have walked a long road together—seven years, two hundred and eighty ayahuasca ceremonies and nineteen shamanic diets thus far. He has been there for me every single step of the way. I know without a doubt that he is the only man in the world who could've helped me and I was guided to him at exactly the right moment. It's no coincidence that I managed to find this guy in the middle of the Amazon jungle, without even knowing I was looking for him.

Words cannot begin to express the depth of my gratitude and love for him. The amount of time and energy that he has devoted to helping me is truly humbling. Hamilton and Don Alberto together have not just saved my life but transformed it beyond my wildest imagination.

"We had to take you on the whole journey," Hamilton says. "All the way from 'Spirits are a load of bollocks' to a direct experience of divinity and *sabiduría divina*" (divine wisdom).

Overcome with emotion, all I can say is, "Thank you, sir. Thank you for your kindness, your patience, your generosity and your friendship."

"You're welcome. It's a pleasure to see how much you've grown. I've got a lot of love for you, Inglés," he says clapping me on the back. "When you go home, remember this: Life is like an ocean. It can seem very turbulent on the surface, but go just a little way down and it's calm. Self is like a cork—always bobbing at the top. Let go of your identity and dive beneath the surface. You may discover that you're the entire ocean."

I notice Don Alberto preparing to leave so I jog over to him to give him a big hug. "*¿Estás arrecho, Inglés?*" he asks and cackles like a Peruvian Sid James. It's the same question he's asked me dozens of times before: "Are you horny, Inglés?"

Alberto departs smiling, and I continue my wanderings, dishing out hugs to friends old and new alike. My soft, smooth skin soaks up the warmth of physical connection. At the same time that I was having my revelations, my skin was undergoing a transformation. I know that the improvements are permanent because the medicine was acting on the underlying condition. There's considerably less sickness in my nervous system. Even my swollen lymph nodes have shrunk.

While a small percentage of the illness remains, I wholeheartedly trust and accept that it's not yet time for me to be entirely free of it. It is time to go home and integrate the ceremonial experiences into my daily life, start living the realisations that I've had over the last several weeks. My work now is to fully inhabit my body and maintain awareness in every moment—the keys to health and wellbeing, not to mention peace, love and a whole lot of fun.

CHAPTER 14
The Search Ends with a New Journey

It's the height of summer back home. I'm looking forward to a few months of warm weather, until I remember that I live in England where I'm met by torrential rain. As the plane makes a wobbly landing at Birmingham Airport, the large, tattooed man next to me whimpers like a schoolgirl before regaining his composure and cursing the pilot.

At home, the astrology books are waiting for me. Like a five-year-old on Christmas morning, I madly tear open the packaging. I read the first book in a day. It's everything I was hoping it would be and more. The way the author describes the subject makes total sense to me.

The amount of information a birth chart contains is staggering. I come across a website that draws up free charts and create one for myself, Rosie, and various family and friends. I read all of the other books and relate them to the printouts that I now have. I can (and do) stare at the charts for hours. Their intricate design and symbols are captivating. The spatial patterns and analytical side of the subject are a perfect fit with the way my mind works. I feel like astrology was made just for me. A surge of energy enlivens me whenever I recognise a characteristic of a chart and understand how it relates to the person's life or identity.

Astrology is not some vague superstitious nonsense. It is solid, accurate information—all there, laid out for you, if you know what you're looking for. I'm astonished that I never knew about all it until now. Of course, pre-ayahuasca Mark would never have been able to understand how astrology could possibly work. He would have called it a load of old hippie bullshit.

For post-ayahuasca Mark, however, it has opened a new doorway. As I sit on my bed, surrounded by a mass of books and birth charts, the realisation hits me: I have found my calling in life—I am going to be an astrologer! Even though I have no idea about the practical side of earning a living from it, I have absolute trust that the finances will work themselves out. The resonance I feel deep in my core leaves me with not a shred of doubt.

I always knew that my time in the jungle would lead to a radically new life. I never knew how that would look, and I even stopped worrying about it. I hadn't given my future career a single thought in a very long time. Then, out of nowhere, "bam!" here it is. It's just as Mimi had predicted four years ago: "When you find what it is that you're meant to do, it'll be exactly what you want to do. It'll be perfect and you will love doing it."

Three years ago, Chris also told me that one day I would help people through working with them on a one-to-one basis. I never thought that there was any work out there that could inspire me in the way astrology does. I know in my heart that I've found something that I will love to do for the rest of my life.

I do a little jig around my bedroom before collapsing onto my bed, laughing at how simultaneously wonderful and ridiculous life is. Lying there beaming, I realise now why I've been attending Toastmasters meetings for the past seven months—the communication skills that I've been honing are essential for this line of work. I'm impressed by how much my confidence and ability to communicate effectively with people has improved, which extends beyond speaking in front of a group to every interaction I have in my daily life. On top of that, it's also a great way to express that part of me that enjoys being the centre of attention—a part that was buried beneath many layers of fear for far too long.

* * *

On the Saturday after I get back from Peru, Rosie and I go for a day's canoeing on the River Severn. It feels like a lifetime has passed since I've seen her. But as we embrace, it feels like we were never apart.

The morning begins with a heavy downpour that enlivens the senses and removes any lingering jetlag. Rosie is wearing a vivid, multicoloured jacket that would make even Timmy Mallett wince. Even so, she still manages to look cute.

The many ducks and geese seem unconcerned by the gentle splash of the paddles as we make our way downstream. The flower-bedecked gardens that back onto the river illustrate the very best of the British countryside. I wave to the fishermen waiting patiently on the river bank and take a deep lungful of fresh air. Something about water has an instant calming effect on me. I sink into a state of deep relaxation. I could do this forever. Rosie and I paddle in synch, deftly avoiding the fishing lines and overhanging branches.

Back at her house, she changes into a flowery summer dress. Emanating radiance and beauty as she walks down the stairs, she takes my hand and leads me out into the field opposite her house. We lie together in silence.

"I want to tell you something," she says after a while. I turn my gaze from the sky to meet hers. She glances away and back again in that coy way that I find so irresistible. "I love you," she says.

"I love you too," I reply and pull her body close to mine.

We lie in each other's arms until the sun sets. Only the chill of the evening forces us inside. Rosie sighs contentedly and wonders aloud: "How does anybody ever get anything done?"

I have no idea.

* * *

SHEDDING THE LAYERS

In the weeks and months that follow, I'm remarkably content with whatever I'm doing. I pester Rosie less and give her the space that she needs. She, in turn, wants to spend more time together. We begin to explore our mutual deepest fear. Surprisingly, I'm not in the least bit scared of sex any more. My work with ayahuasca was paramount. It also helps that this is Rosie's first experience. I feel no pressure to be any sort of expert, which leaves us free to discover the magic of the act together.

"You're very good at this," she whispers to me.

What on earth was I ever worried about?

As we continue to grow closer, I must remain ever vigilant not to slip back into old patterns. The ayahuasca has served to highlight areas of my behaviour that do not contribute to my well-being. It has made me starkly aware of the obsessive nature of my mind, and how it is never satiated with what I have. Ayahuasca has helped me become more accepting, calmer and happier, but it hasn't entirely stopped my mind from grasping for more.

While ayahuasca has helped me change drastically in some ways, astrology has shown me that my fundamental nature is fixed. I will always have a powerful and compulsive mind with an attention to fine details, often overlooked by others. Therefore, I must ensure that I embody the higher expression of this energy, for example, by using it to gain a deep understanding of astrology, thereby helping others to fulfil their potential. The alternative is allowing my mind to be in control, obsessing over minutiae and criticising others, especially Rosie. "The mind is a wonderful tool but a terrible boss," as Chris once said.

It is futile to wish that she or I were any other way. The only resolution is love. Love Rosie exactly as she is. Love my life exactly as it is. Love my mind and its feverish thoughts exactly as they are.

Rosie was absolutely right when she said that what I was looking for in her I already have inside of me. I've seen it in ceremony. I may not experience the all-encompassing love that is forever in my heart on a daily basis, but I know it's in there.

The testing nature of our relationship notwithstanding, we both sense a deep connection, well beyond anything that could be explained rationally. Rosie feels that she has known me in a previous life. She, just like Hamilton, has come into my life at the exact moment I needed her—not necessarily to give me everything I want; to guide me through the next stage of my spiritual growth. Her presence again illuminates the magical synchronicities of life. She is a reminder that every moment of every day happens exactly as it should, when it should. This is the perfection of the Universe.

A friend said recently that the best relationships are often the ones that push our buttons because there's no chance of growth in a mutual admiration society. After being with Rosie I completely get it. Despite our differences, which do bring up challenges, we understand one another and can talk honestly about everything. I appreciate the openness of our communication. It's the key to our evolution as individuals and our strength as a couple. To be honest though, I quite like the sound of the mutual admiration society—gazing dreamily into each other's eyes for hours on end, oblivious to the existence of an outside world.

* * *

I start a daily yoga practice for an hour each morning to help me stay present throughout the day. It also contributes to the strengthening and cleansing of my body. As I lie this morning in Relaxation Pose, relishing the energy flowing throughout my body, I remember the dream in which I rode the giant white horse off into the sunset. I'm certainly moving closer to it. Yet, there's plenty of work still to do. Regardless, my spirit is awakening. That horse and I have surfaced from beneath the water and are now riding atop the ocean.

Yoga is one small part of my new life, a life that will be made up of many small, unremarkable parts. Mindful living is a way of life that will revolutionise my being in a gentle and subtle, yet solid and real manner over the coming months and years. Ayahuasca has pointed the way. The rest is up to me.

Another feature of my new life is football. In the dusky light of a Birmingham park, I control the long pass from my teammate and turn past the defender in the same movement. Without needing so much as a sight of goal, I slide the ball under the keeper's advancing body and wait for the satisfying sound of ball hitting net. I'm greeted with silence. I look up to see the ball disappearing into the distance. My shot was at least six feet wide of the target. Nonetheless, I smile contentedly. Now that I'm thirty-seven years old my chances of playing for England are looking slim. Maybe that dream of playing for Aston Villa could still come true though.

Regardless, I've become one of those people who used to mystify me—someone who knows that reality is better than any dream. That's *because* of the illness, not in spite of it. When I recall what I love about my life, which I remind myself to do often, I see it has come as a direct result of the sickness: a beautiful girlfriend, a new career that is just perfect for me and excites me every time I think about it, numerous close and loving friends and a sense of peace, love and trust in the divine nature of existence. What more could I ask for, really?

My quest was vital to address the sadness, loneliness, fear and low self-esteem that had concealed the true radiance of my being.

Now that ayahuasca has shown me the truth and helped free me from my fears and self-doubt, I'd rather have died than have to live my pre-ayahuasca life, even if I were completely healthy. The mild physical discomfort I currently live with is infinitely preferable to the mental torment I suffered throughout the years.

Finally, I've found the missing piece I've been searching for—the awareness of my own divinity and with it, a direct connection with love/God/my heart/the Universe. I always had this connection and always will. At the same time, I have confirmed that there is a whole lot more to life than I could sense. The Spirit World is just as real as this one. It contains an endless number of spirit guides and helpers who are waiting to assist in all aspects of daily life.

More than seven years after my ordeal began all that remains is a minor form of eczema. Since my last visit to Blue Morpho, I no longer take the immunosuppressants. And I only use a little bit of steroid cream now and then. Overall, everything is fantastic. Actually, it's more than fantastic—everything is absolutely bloody marvellous.

I'm still prone to forget the wisdom and divine knowledge I acquired in Peru. I can get frustrated when I'm stuck in traffic. I can sulk when I don't get my own way with Rosie, and I can revert to being a stroppy teenager when I'm with my parents. But the wisdom and knowledge I've gained haven't disappeared. In those moments, I've simply forgotten about them. As soon as I relax and become present, I remember. And when I remember, I laugh like a young child at the magnificence of existence.

* * *

The face looking back at me in the mirror is serene, the skin flawless, and the eyes alert and eager after a peaceful night's sleep.

SHEDDING THE LAYERS

I yawn and stretch extravagantly. A delicious warmth fills my body. Vitality courses through my torso and down into my arms and legs. A wide smile breaks out on my face at the thought of the day ahead.

On the surface, there's nothing special or different about today. It's just another ordinary Thursday. I will do my yoga routine, work a little, study some astrology and spend time with people I love. It's a day that begins with remembering that simply being alive is a miracle. Suddenly the day doesn't feel quite so ordinary.

I take a deep breath and reach for the nearest shirt.

ABOUT THE AUTHOR

Mark Flaherty lives in England and works as an astrologer with an international client base. Find out more and schedule a reading on his website: www.mark-flaherty.com